The Balancing Act

Arminianism v. Calvinism

Dr. Daniel F. Beckley, Th. D.

Forward by
Dr. Randy White

The Balancing Act

Arminianism v. Calvinism

Dr. Daniel F. Beckley, Th. D.

Copyright © 2007
All rights reserved

Dr. Daniel F. Beckley retains all rights to this book. Contents of this book may not be reproduced in part or its entirety, with the exception of review purposes, without obtaining written permission from Dr. Beckley.

Published by Painted Word Studios
Crosby, Texas, USA
1 866 251-7510

Cover art design by Eve Thornton

Contact Dr. Beckley
www.danielbeckley.com
dfbeckley@danielbeckley.com

Manufactured in the United States of America

For His honor and His glory

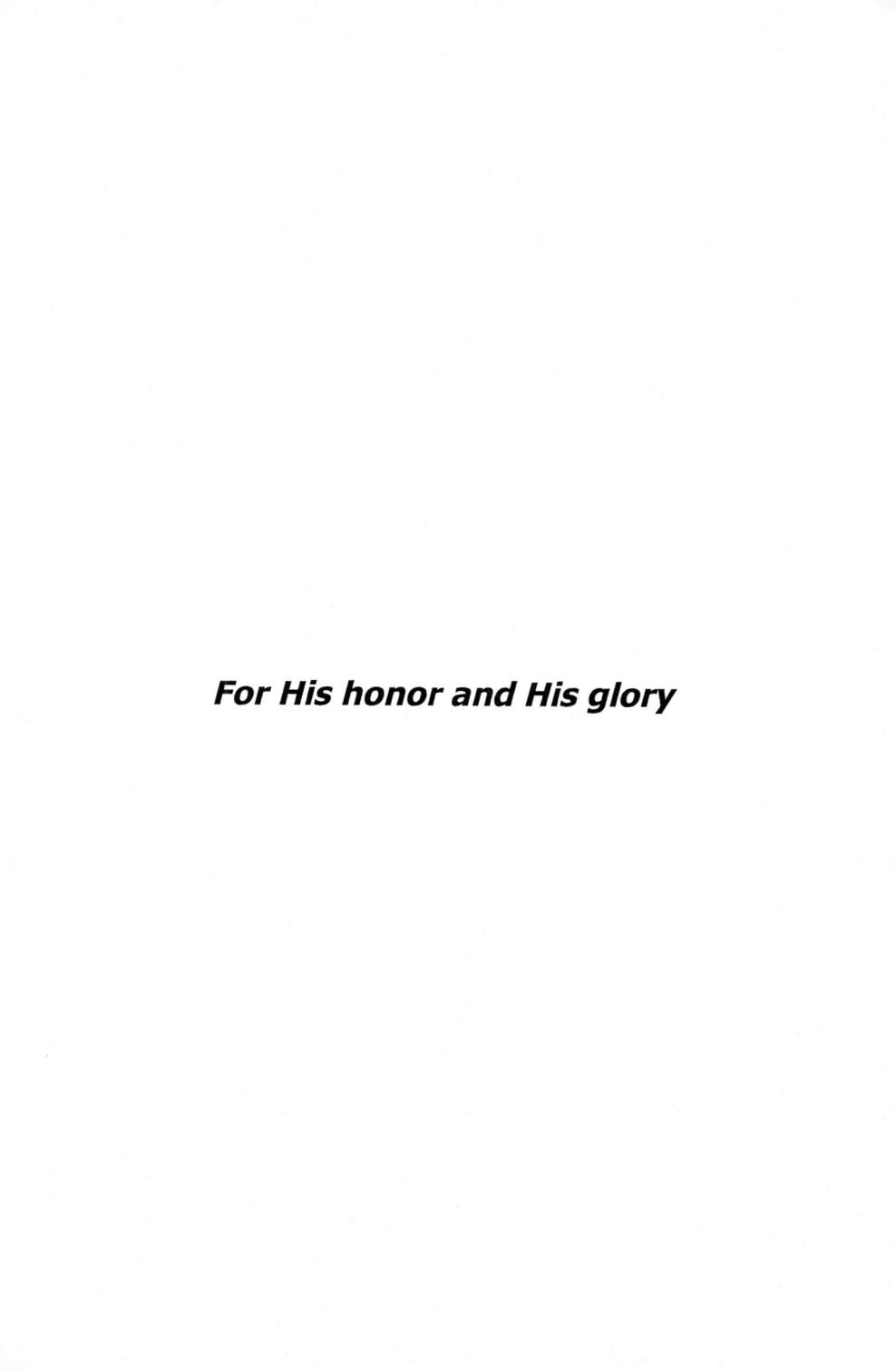

Forward

Congratulations on proving yourself to be a deep thinker by determining to read this book! As you read this book you will hear the mind of a man who has faithfully worked to lay out issues of a debate that has lasted for almost five centuries and has handle them with both clarity and fairness.

It is rare that an individual can take a well-debated issue, look at the myriad of viewpoints, and attempt to present a conclusion that satisfies both Scripture and human reason. This is exactly what Dan Beckley has attempted to do in this work.

No one would suppose that any new work will put to rest a debate that has been raging for hundreds of years, and Dr. Beckley doesn't pretend that this volume will achieve such a feat. What the author does expect is to provide the layman with a rich resource that will enable understanding of a very complex issue. He achieves this goal skillfully, without boring the reader with irrelevant issues or by confusing the reader with endless trivialities. The Balancing Act achieves its intent — providing a "fair and balanced" conclusion to one of the church's most difficult and longest points of debate.

As you read, know that you are reading the words of a man whose life is committed to a mentoring style of discipleship. Nothing thrills the soul of Dan Beckley more than the God-given privilege of taking a learner by the spiritual hand and leading them to a clearer understanding that will exhibit measurable growth. Dr. Beckley's interest is the human soul and that soul's relationship to and the understanding of its Creator. He is a stated literalist, a faithful churchman, a thoughtful teacher, and a practical theologian. He can discuss theology over-lunch or in front of a classroom of hungry listeners. His theology grows out of his love for Jesus, His service through the church, and His commitment to the Word of God.

Reading this book and studying the issue at hand can, I believe, provide great encouragement in your walk, as well as growth in your understanding of Scripture. Take each chapter prayerfully and live each truth faithfully. My prayer is that as you dive into the truths of this book that your understanding of God's Truth would set you free!

Dr. Randy White
Pastor, First Baptist Church
Katy, Texas

With Thanks

God has blessed me so much by surrounding me with Godly people who have such tender hearts. Without the inspiration of the Holy Spirit and the affirmation of many people, this book would never have been realized. I thank my Pastor, Dr. Randy White, who has graciously written the forward to this book. I thank my friend and the first pastor under whom I have served, Dr. Carl Lenz, who encouraged me and to this day still reminds me that as "Iron Sharpens Iron – So One Man Sharpens Another", as read in Proverbs 27:17. I praise God for the men, strong Christian brothers, who have listened to my sometimes 'half-baked' ideas and challenged them when they needed "more baking". It is friends like the men of our Cross-Talk Sunday School Class, Phil Cooper, Chic Coonrod, Chuck Allen, Gene Campbell and, my best (earthly) friend, Jim Mick, who have shared their strong faith, their testimonies of Christ, and their hearts with me. I thank God for my five children, who have listened to Dad pounding away on Sunday School lessons, sermons and this manuscript, and my wife, Carolyn, who has held the position of being my sounding board – making sure that the idea that I'm trying to convey is made clear. But most of all, I thank my Lord and Savior, Jesus Christ, for the free gift of salvation that is found only in Him – by grace, through faith.

Introduction

It amazes me how hard-headed, intransigent and unwilling to change people are. We are creatures of habit and are so comfortable in holding on to our positions. We hate things that move us out of that comfort zone. There's only one problem with this comfort zone, theologically speaking, and that problem is made manifest when it is not consistent with God's plan for our lives.

I have observed people in today's 'modern church' who are looking to find a 'contemporary Jesus'. They search for a Christ of convenience, not the true Sovereign God of the Bible. They want a Christ that is relevant to today, neither one steeped in Jewish context nor one that is 2000 years old. This approach cannot be judged consistent with God's plan for our lives either.

I recently saw a quote on a church billboard that spoke volumes. It simply said, "Stop trying to change the message! The message is supposed to be changing you!" This is really at the crux of all theological debates and social issues – our struggle to make God conform to our desires rather than our willing conformance to His desires. We ascribe to God certain characteristics – His wisdom, His love, His mercy, His grace – yet we ignore His desire for us to become the absolute best we can be. We fail to acknowledge that He wants us to change because it will require us to move out of that comfort zone.

One of the reasons we fail to recognize the need to change is because there are false impressions about

God, propagated by a lost world, presenting a lost world-view of God. The only way to correct this deficiency is to pursue a **deep, fresh, and honest study of the character of God**. One such study could focus on the in-house (within the church) dispute between those of the "Arminian / Free Will" position and those of the "Calvinist / Limited Atonement" position. To accomplish a study of these positions, it is a requirement to have a clear and concise understanding of the true character of God and how *inter-dependent* His character truly is.

It is that clear and concise understanding that this book is intended to provoke. While this manuscript offers a third option, the reader is encouraged to use this study to gain a deeper understanding of the Sovereign Lord of this universe. **Clearly, He, and not man, must be the objective of the study – for salvation must begin and end with God**. The finite mind of man will always be challenged when trying to comprehend the infinite God. However, we must strive to gain more knowledge of the great and glorious provider of our salvation. This book is not written for scholarly approval, but to assist the person who sits in the pew to understand that God must always be found as Sovereign *AND* Gracious. My prayer is that we both gain greater insight in the character of our Lord.

Daniel F. Beckley
Houston, Texas
2007

Table of Contents

Chapter Title

1	The Debate
2	The Nature of God & Man
3	The Position of Calvinists
4	The Free Will Position
5	We Need A Third Option
6	Truth or Consequences
7	Specific Conflict
8	More Conflict
9	Premises & Promises
10	Confusion & Complications
11	God To The Rescue
12	Confusing Catechisms
13	God Is In Control
14	The Third Option
15	The Balancing Act
16	A Sovereign God
17	The Best Choice
18	The Best Option
19	Afterward

Chapter 1

The Debate

The debate has raged over the years, through many generations of scholars, from before the time of the Reformation to today's modern theology, on the question of eternal security in salvation. It is an issue that has been divisive and, at times, even explosive. The outcry in favor of or in opposition to eternal security raises questions about the character of God and the nature of man, with each position equally dependent upon our perception of the nature of God and the character of man. Within the arena of ideas, debate on this issue is nominally found to be quite emotional and usually closed-minded. Man is somehow required to choose or, as a result of not making a choice, being labeled with one of the two position identities.

This document puts forth data from which the opposing doctrines are developed. I will submit for your evaluation that, with both of these doctrines drawn from the same Divinely Inspired Scripture, God cannot be as confusing as these two divergent points would suggest about a subject so vital and central to Christian theology.

In this presentation, all Scriptural references are taken from the _Authorized Version (AV) of the Bible_, translated by order of King James, with subsequent revisions, unless otherwise noted. To show the basis of each position, I am utilizing tables and descriptive references from *The Moody Handbook of Theology*, Moody Press, Chicago, 1989, as they have done such a wonderful work of presenting the two positions.

I would remind the reader that these two positions (Calvinism & Arminianism) reflect the opinion of man and may not necessarily reflect the Divine position correctly. I believe wholeheartedly that God cannot be the "author of confusion" as 1st Corinthians 14:33 clearly states and that He therefore would not, could not, be the originator of this heated debate of such dramatic proportions. In the Second Epistle to the church at Corinth, Chapter 11, Paul gives us some interesting verses for our consideration.

> *^{1} Would to God ye could bear with me a little in my folly: and indeed bear with me. ^{2} For I am jealous over you with godly jealousy: for I have espoused you to one husband, that I may present you as a chaste virgin to Christ. ^{3} But I fear, lest by any means, as the serpent beguiled Eve through his subtlety, so your minds should be* **corrupted from the simplicity that is in Christ**.

Paul knew that there would be occasions where things would get more complicated than they should. He knew that man would make a muddle of the simplicity of the Good News that is found in Jesus Christ. He knew because he was penning the Epistle at the direction of the Holy Spirit. Our loving Father gave us the truth of His Living Word, Jesus Christ, in a continuous fashion, delivered from Genesis through Revelation. Each and every possible doctrinal position, no matter how dramatic or inconsequential, must be evaluated in light

The Balancing Act

of the simplicity that is found in Jesus Christ. But be sure that you understand that this simplicity is founded, not in the weakness of the Lord, but in the spiritual limitations, confusion and blindness of sinful man. As God's revelation progresses, the picture should become clearer, yet, unfortunately, this debate has produced the opposite result. Perhaps we need fewer theologians and more men who are willing to receive God's Word at face value.

As we study God's Word, we must be open to the working of the Holy Spirit. We must prayerfully seek God's wisdom. In James' Epistle, Chapter 1, we are provided with some extremely good advice. The advice that we receive from the Word of God is so simple and of such beauty that we should learn to ask the Lord for understanding and **_trust Him_** – without confusion. Remember, God isn't the author of confusion, Satan is.

> [5] **_If any of you lack wisdom, let him ask of God, that giveth to all men liberally, and upbraideth not; and it shall be given him_**. [6] **_But let him ask in faith, nothing wavering_**. *For he that wavereth is like a wave of the sea driven with the wind and tossed.* [7] *For let not that man think that he shall receive any thing of the Lord.*

Unless you are willing to ask the Lord for His wisdom, which is another way of saying that you want to know His doctrine, you cannot see the clarity of His doctrine that is necessary to grow in grace and knowledge of our Lord, Jesus Christ. We should always remember that the real teacher is the Holy Spirit.

Dr. Daniel F. Beckley

Let's establish some of the theological points that we will encounter in our study, for the purpose of developing our own doctrine. In the ultimate test of doctrine, remember, it is the precept of the Lord that must have the preeminence over the opinion of man. We will discuss:

1. The Nature of God
2. The Nature of Man
3. The Character of God
4. The Character of Man
5. Option #1 - The Position of Calvinism
6. Option #2 - The Free Will Position
7. A Possible Third Option

Chapter 2
The Nature of God & Man

The Nature of God – Unchanging Eternally
The nature of God does not require a great deal of clarification. We know from Scripture that the Lord has an unchanging nature (Malachi 3:6, James 1:17, etc...). What must be considered is how that nature interacts with the character of God. For instance, if God reveals through His Word that Jesus Christ died simply because He is "not willing that any should perish, but that all should come to repentance", His very nature refutes any possible consideration of any predetermined condition of man whereby 'some' would not be able to be saved. The conflict with the nature of God, mathematically speaking, is a 'null set'. It cannot occur and since it cannot occur, any doctrine that is founded in part or whole cannot stand the Divine test. The specifics of how His nature negates certain possibilities will be addressed in 'A Third Option'.

The Nature of Man – Unchanging Mortal Flesh
An inescapable truth is the sinful nature of man. Since the fall of Adam, when sin was first known by man, each man born has been unable to escape the reality of the 'X and Y Chromosome Factor', the sin nature. Science has revealed the wisdom of God with respect to the determination of gender. Hence we have the passing on of the sinful nature of man exhibited by the transmission of Chromosomes. Consider that the X or Y Chromosome contributed by the male combines with the X Chromosome that the female donates. The process produces only two possible outcomes, with 'XX'

producing a female and 'XY' producing a male. No other combination can be the result. This sin nature is transmitted from generation to generation, not by the 'dictated punishment by God,' but by the wonder of God (each child is 'fearfully and wonderfully made – Psalm 139:14). Jesus Christ Himself was wonderfully made, but, even more fearfully, because His 'Y' Chromosome came via the Holy Spirit from the Heavenly Father. That is one of the undeniable facts that made Jesus Christ able to break the bondage of sin. Although His earthly mother, Mary, was of the seed of Adam, it is the glorious way that the Father chose to set man free from sin – through the virgin birth of His Son. In the "Immaculate Conception," the Divine nature of God (through the determining 'Y' Chromosome) is passed on to the Son of God rather than the carnal nature of man.

Conversely, by transmission of the gender specific 'X' & 'Y' Chromosome from the earthly father to an earthly child, man transmits the sin nature. The sin nature is that carnal desire to please self. <u>Sin, as a contrast to sin nature, is anything that man does which is contrary to the revealed Word of God or the character & nature of God.</u> God could not permit the transmission of a sinful nature into the Savior of the world. Man's nature cannot change as long as he is in the flesh (he can only change the tendency, the pattern). God had to intervene because of the war between the spirit and the flesh. The apostle Paul wrote extensively, over in Romans 5, 6, 7 and 8, on the warlike condition that exists in a redeemed man, as carnal flesh rebels against the spirit. Christ could not have that rebellion in

Himself or He would not have been an acceptable sacrifice.

The Character of God – Unchanging Eternally

Those who have possessed the hunger for God's Word have searched exhaustively to find the true character of God. In His Word, we find that Christ is the visible image of the invisible God (Colossians 1:15) and that God is Omnipotent (Revelation 19:6), Omnipresent (Psalm 46:1), Omniscient (1 John 3:20), Eternal (1 Timothy 1:17), Gracious (Exodus 34:6), Faithful (Daniel 9:4), Loving (Romans 5:5), and many more things that man would desire to be. Perhaps most important in the character of God is His righteousness (Exodus 9:27), for this is the character trait that says that although the Lord knows the difference between 'good' and 'evil' (Genesis 3:22), the Lord has never considered to do anything even remotely considered 'evil'. It is not simply His pondering over a subject and then rejecting the incorrect (sinful) thing and choosing the correct (righteous) thing to do, it is that God because His righteous character will not even entertain the evil thought. The possibility of choosing to do 'evil' is made nought. This is the essence of His righteous character. This is the part of His character that demands a payment for sin – complete atonement for sin, in love, not just payment for injury that sin costs.

The Character of Man – Changing Through Sanctification

Whether man desires it or not, the Lord wants us to work with Him to change our character. This is what is called to process of sanctification. It is an integral part of salvation. At the moment of salvation, man can stand justified before the Lord, seen through the blood of Jesus Christ as His righteousness is imputed to us. II Corinthians 5:21 tells us, "For he hath made him to be sin for us, who knew no sin; that we might be made the righteousness of God in him." This is the vehicle that God chose to use for man to be able to overcome the flesh and the carnal, selfish way of living. This is the vehicle that Romans 8:29 relates as we read, "For whom he did foreknow, <u>He also did predestinate to be conformed to the image of his Son</u>, that he might be the firstborn among many brethren." Changing the character of man through the process of sanctification is the molding of man into the image of Jesus Christ on the potter's wheel of God. The molding process takes place via two separate, yet linked tools called trial and temptation. Consider the simplified comparison of the two:

Trial	**Temptation**
Provided by God	Permitted by God
Originated by God	Originated by Satan
To Test Faith	To Test Righteousness

While temptation is the means by which man's righteousness is tested and thus sanctification's progress is evaluated, it is by faith, trusting in God's Word, by which a man withstands temptation. 1st Corinthians, Chapter 10, provides the Scriptural reference for this position.

> [11] *Now all these things happened unto them for ensamples: and they are written for our admonition, upon whom the ends of the world are come.* [12] *Wherefore let him that thinketh he standeth take*

heed lest he fall. ¹³ *There hath no temptation taken you but such as is common to man: <u>but God is faithful, who will not suffer you to be tempted above that ye are able; but will with the temptation also make a way to escape, that ye may be able to bear it</u>.*

As the passage reveals, it is by faith that we stand in the righteousness of Jesus Christ. Our faith in God's provision of the means of escape is spoken of in verse 13 and it is the key to withstanding the temptation. It is that ability to stand firm in faith, just as the Lord Jesus Christ did in His temptation that is available to us. This is the tool of escape that the Lord promises. All we have to do is to rely on the truth of Scripture, just as the Lord did (Matthew 4, Luke 4). Our faith, in recalling the promises of God and our experience of His faithfulness affords man the confidence to do the right thing, choosing the way of God through the Word of God. The final result is that our righteousness (our progress in sanctification - being conformed to the image of Jesus) is tested. When we pass that test, our righteousness is validated while our faith is strengthened, all through the comfort we find in the Word of God.

Dr. Daniel F. Beckley

Chapter 3

The Position of Calvinism

On one side of the debate on security of salvation we find those who are called 'Calvinists'. These individuals have doctrinal affirmations based upon the unavoidable call of God and overwhelming grace of God to defend the principle of eternal security. Calvinism is also known as Reformed faith and is historically used as the identifier between the adherents of this doctrine, as well as to those of the Lutheran and the Anabaptist persuasion. The beginning of Calvinism is expressed in papers called the *Institutes of Christian Religion*. The writings of John Calvin (1509-1564) are his rejection of what he referred to as "superstitions of the Papacy", Roman Catholicism. Most people define Calvinism through five general points, called *TULIP*, although there are other teachings that are inherent to Calvinist doctrine. The five general points of Calvinism are:

- **Total Depravity of Man** – As a result of Adam's fall, the entire human race is affected; all humanity is dead in trespasses and sin. Man is unable to save himself.

- **Unconditional Election** – Because man is dead in sin, he is unable to initiate a response to God; therefore, in eternity past God elected certain people to salvation. Election and predestination are unconditional; they are not based on man's response.

- **Limited Atonement** – Because God determined that certain ones should be saved as a result of God's unconditional election; He determined that Christ should die for the elect. All whom God has elected and Christ died for will be saved.

- **Irresistible Grace** – Those whom God elected and Christ died for; God draws to Himself through irresistible grace. God makes man willing to come to Him. When God calls, man responds.

- **Perseverance of the Saints** – The precise ones God has elected and drawn to Himself through the Holy Spirit will persevere in faith. None whom God has elected will be lost; they are eternally secure.

These five points summarize the Calvinist viewpoint but it does not explain all aspects of John Calvin's personal doctrine. Due to limitations of space, I have not included discussion of the other points of Calvinist doctrine. Suffice to say that this is similar to the fact that Martin Luther's doctrine was not limited to the subject of plenary indulgences (paying earthly sums of money for entry of loved ones into heaven). In looking at the ideals of Calvinism, several key questions beg for the asking – but we will ask those later under the heading called "***The Third Option***."

Chapter 4

The Free Will Position

The Opinion of Arminius

Jacobus Arminius (1560-1609) was a Dutch theologian who originally followed the tenets of John Calvin. That was until he observed a debate in Geneva, Switzerland that pitted Beza (Calvin's son-in-law) against Koornheert, a man who was opposed to all that Calvin taught. Arminius found that Koornheert was better able to defend his position than Beza and the explanations of Koornheert provoked Arminius to begin searching the Scriptures for God's truth. Several faithful followers who presented these views after Jacobus Arminius' death in a document called the _Remonstrance_ in 1610.

The doctrine promoted by Arminius' views is essentially the Free Will doctrine promoted in churches such as Free Will Baptist, Church of Christ, and some Pentecostal denominations. The doctrine utilizes eight points to state the essential doctrine in lieu of the five points of Calvinism (_TULIP_). The following is a summary of the eight points.

Doctrine	Arminianism	Calvinism
Depravity	As a result of the Fall, man has inherited a corrupted nature. Prevenient grace has removed the guilt and condemnation of Adam's sin.	As a result of the Fall, man is totally depraved and dead in his sin; he is unable to save himself. Because he is dead in sin, God must initiate salvation.

Dr. Daniel F. Beckley

Doctrine	Arminianism	Calvinism
Imputation of Sin	God did not impute sin to the entire human race through Adam's sin, but all people inherit a corrupt nature as a result of Adam's fall.	Through Adam's transgression, sin was imputed – passed to the entire race so that all people are born in sin.
Election	God elected those whom He knew would believe of their own free will. Election is conditional, based on man's response in faith.	God unconditionally, from eternity past, elected some to be saved. Election is not based on man's future response.
Atonement of Christ	Christ died for the entire human race, making all mankind savable. His death is effective only in those who believe.	God determined that Christ would die for all those whom God elected. Since Christ did not die for everyone, but only for those who were elected to be saved, His death is completely successful.
Grace	Through prevenient or preparatory grace, which is given to all people, man is able to cooperate with God and respond to Him in salvation. Prevenient grace reverses the effects of Adam's sin.	Common grace is extended to all mankind but is insufficient to save anyone. Through irresistible grace God drew to Himself those whom He had elected, making them willing to respond.

The Balancing Act

Doctrine	Arminianism	Calvinism
Will of Man	Prevenient grace is given to all people and is exercised on the entire person, giving man a free will.	Depravity extends to all of man, including his will. Without irresistible grace man's will remains bound, unable to respond to God on its own ability
Perseverance	Believers may turn from grace and lose their salvation.	Believers will persevere in the faith. Believers are secure in their salvation; none will be lost.
Sovereignty of God	God limits His control in accord with man's freedom and response. His decrees are related to His foreknowledge of what man's response will be.	God's sovereignty is absolute and unconditional. He has determined all things according to the good pleasure of His will. His foreknowledge originates in advanced planning, not in advanced information.

I find it interesting that there is a sarcastic joke that suggests that those who hold to the Free Will position have their own "TULIP". It simply states, "He loves me, He loves me not. He loves me."

I'll not take the time here to discuss the contrast between the two doctrines in depth since the table speaks well enough on it's own. The table, produced from page 491 of *The Moody Handbook of Theology*, places the matter before you with neither prejudice nor preference. I will address the points of both Calvinism and Arminianism in greater detail during the segment entitled **The Third Option**.

Dr. Daniel F. Beckley

Chapter 5

We Need A Third Option

The choice of the term '***The Third Option***' is not one of great ingenuity, divine inspiration or even an immodest attempt to be thought clever. Whether people admit it or not, unless they are part of a 'hard-shell' faction that openly declares to be either a Calvinist or Arminian, most church members belong to groups that either ignore the debate or they embrace some alternative of their own.

The position of ignorance is one that considers the positions of Calvinism and Arminianism and presents them like the foundation points on the Gateway Arch in St. Louis. Allow each foundation to represent the respective positions of Calvinism and Arminianism, with each foundation of the Arch clearly seen on the shore of the Mississippi River. The key in this allusion is that these foundations can be seen on a very cloudy day. People cannot see precisely where those two sides meet, somewhere above the clouds, but by ignorance they are willing to accept that God has somehow made it all work out. How? They do not care how, but they're willing to accept that it simply does work out.

These members of the third option embrace some parts of a five-point doctrine (Calvinist) or eight-point doctrine (Arminian). However, they reject one or more points within the doctrines due to personal discomfort, weakness of the position on a Scriptural basis, or simply because they have a problem reconciling a specific point with their understanding of the nature and character of God.

Problems reconciling tenets of a given doctrine with the nature and character of God and in conflict with Scripture are the only real reasons to reject any doctrine. Unfortunately, most people reject doctrinal issues on the basis of the first premise (personal discomfort) or personal preference. Perhaps the greatest example of rejecting a doctrinal position on the basis of personal discomfort pertains to the issue of homosexuality, where people do not wish to change lifestyles to conform to the dictates of Scripture or a local New Testament, Bible teaching and Bible believing church. If we accept Romans 8:29 in a literal sense, we must not accept a lifestyle or a doctrine which is clearly contrary to the image of Jesus Christ. Our goal is to come as close to that image as we possibly can - **before** we are called home to glory.

To comprehend which ideas of any doctrine might be contrary to the nature and / or character of God, a believer must seriously pursue knowledge and wisdom of that Divine nature and character. Without this pursuit of wisdom, man cannot possibly arrive at the correct decision, except by mere chance.

At the heart of the discussion of the possible third option is whether salvation is secure as we walk in the flesh. From my study of God's word, I believe that there is nothing that the Lord could do or would be willing to allow in the realm of salvation that would show any deficiency on His part. After all, God is the originator of salvation, as well as the finisher.

Therefore He cannot:

- Have insufficient power to accomplish His task. To place restrictions on the Lord on this point, we would be stating that God is not omnipotent, but possessing only limited power.

- Have insufficient or inadequate grace to call all men to salvation. To deny this is to deny the power and the intent of God.

- Have insufficient mercy, whereby some are, from eternity past, predestinated to an eternity in the lake of fire. To consider this, the Lord would have to be unmerciful.

- Have inadequate forgiveness, whereby some sins cannot be forgiven. To realize that God would be petty and unforgiving again conflicts with the nature of God.

- Be unable to hear the cry for help of someone who is not part of the 'elect'. Again we have a conflict with the merciful nature of God, but this time it places God in the position of ignoring the call from one of His created beings.

Man's Worst Destiny

Man must bear the responsibility for his own eternal destiny. This statement does not limit God's role in salvation, but it does have everything to do with whether a man or woman can make salvation of no effect. My comments here, supported extensively in Scripture, indicate that if a man does not receive eternal life, it is not because of any fault of the Lord. The character and nature of God is such that by defining the Lord as omnipotent, omniscient and omnipresent, we preclude any area of salvation doctrine by which man can fall short of salvation through the direct action of the Lord. Herein lies the dilemma that man does not wish to address, for if there is anything that can fall short of God's plan, it rests squarely with men and women. In the equation of salvation, man and woman are responsible if failure to receive salvation occurs.

Chapter 6

Truth or Consequences

Let's look at some statements, without classifying whether Calvinist or Arminian in nature, and provide some comment about how these statements reflect on the nature and character of God and consider them in light of the Scripture.

- **The sovereignty of God is an absolute & totally unconditional in this temporal world.**

- **Predestination, foreknowledge & election are all the same thing.**

- **Salvation requires a faith covenant.**

- **God's grace is limited.**

- **God's general grace removes the guilt and condemnation of Adam's sin.**

- **God's saving grace is different from God's general grace.**

- **God's grace is sufficient for some, but not for all.**

- **God's grace is irresistible for some but not for others.**

- **Man's free will is not associated with salvation in any manner.**

- **God cannot save all men and women.**

- **God's plan of salvation did not include all of man.**

- **God dictates that a man must go to an eternity of torment without ever hearing the Word of God or having the chance of salvation.**

- **Jesus' sacrifice is not completely successful because not all men will be saved.**

- **People, who have tasted the goodness of the Lord, can reject the faith covenant, and lose their salvation, with the result of spending eternity in the Lake of Fire.**

While these are not the only questions that need to be answered before we draw our final conclusion, they give insight, in my opinion, as to how men can misinterpret the character and nature of God, while denying the true nature of man. We'll deal with these specific questions as we examine the Arminian and Calvinistic positions and then explore the questions as we consider the implications of a third option.

As we consider the logical extensions of the positions suggested by the Arminian and Calvinist doctrines, we will explore Scripture verses that speak to these specific points. After viewing these positions, we'll contrast them with the character and nature of the Lord. Let's bring back our eight-point comparison table.

The Balancing Act

Doctrine	Arminian	Calvinism
Depravity	As a result of the Fall, man has inherited a corrupted nature. Prevenient grace has removed the guilt and condemnation of Adam's sin.	As a result of the Fall, man is totally depraved and dead in his sin; he is unable to save himself. Because he is dead in sin, God must initiate salvation.
Imputation of Sin	God did not impute sin to the entire human race through Adam's sin, but all people inherit a corrupt nature as a result of Adam's fall.	Through Adam's transgression, sin was imputed – passed to the entire race so that all people are born in sin.
Election	God elected those whom He knew would believe of their own free will. Election is conditional, based on man's response in faith.	God unconditionally, from eternity past, elected some to be saved. Election is not based on man's future response.
Atonement of Christ	Christ died for the entire human race, making all mankind savable. His death is effective only in those who believe.	God determined that Christ would die for all those whom God elected. Since Christ did not die for everyone, but only for those who were elected to be saved, His death is completely successful.

Doctrine	Arminian	Calvinism
Grace	Through prevenient or preparatory grace, which is given to all people, man is able to cooperate with God and respond to Him in salvation. Prevenient grace reverses the effects of Adam's sin.	Common grace is extended to all mankind but is insufficient to save anyone. Through irresistible grace God drew to Himself those whom He had elected, making them willing to respond.
Will of Man	Prevenient grace is given to all people and is exercised on the entire person, giving man a free will.	Depravity extends to all of man, including his will. Without irresistible grace man's will remains bound, unable to respond to God on its own ability
Perseverance	Believers may turn from grace and lose their salvation.	Believers will persevere in the faith. Believers are secure in their salvation; none will be lost.
Sovereignty of God	God limits His control in accord with man's freedom and response. His decrees are related to His foreknowledge of what man's response will be.	God's sovereignty is absolute and unconditional. He has determined all things according to the good pleasure of His will. His foreknowledge originates in advanced planning, not in advanced information.

Chapter 7

Specific Conflict

Looking at the specific statements of the doctrinal positions, let's examine and qualify whether the statement is valid and whether it is possible to establish a doctrine from the Lord's perspective.

As a result of the Fall, man has inherited a corrupted nature. Prevenient grace has removed the guilt and condemnation of Adam's sin. This is the first statement of the Arminian (Free Will) position. At first glance, it appears to be valid, but does it permit the full confidence from which doctrine may be established? I believe that it lacks full confidence from several perspectives.

First, consider that as a result of the fall (Adam's sin), man inherits a corrupt nature. Do we inherit a corrupt nature? Let's see what the Word of God has to say. In Genesis 3:9-24, we find " *⁹ And the LORD God called unto Adam, and said unto him, where art thou? ¹⁰ And he said, **I heard thy voice in the garden, and I was afraid, because I was naked; and I hid myself**. ¹¹ And he said, who told thee that thou wast naked? Hast thou eaten of the tree, whereof I commanded thee that thou shouldest not eat? ¹² And the man said, **the woman whom thou gavest to be with me, she gave me of the tree, and I did eat**. ¹³ And the LORD God said unto the woman, what is this that thou hast done? And the woman said, the serpent beguiled me, and I did eat. ¹⁴ And the LORD God said unto the serpent, Because thou hast done this, thou art* cursed above all cattle, and above every beast of the field; upon thy belly shalt thou go, and dust shalt thou eat all the days of thy life: [15] And I will put enmity between thee and the woman, and between thy seed and her seed; it shall bruise thy head, and thou shalt bruise his heel. [16] **Unto the woman he said, I will greatly multiply thy sorrow and thy conception; in sorrow thou shalt bring forth children**; and thy desire shall be to thy husband, and he shall rule over thee. [17] And unto Adam he said, **Because thou hast hearkened unto the voice of thy wife, and hast eaten of the tree, of which I commanded thee, saying, Thou shalt not eat of it: cursed is the ground for thy sake; in sorrow shalt thou eat of it all the days of thy life**; [18] Thorns also and thistles shall it bring forth to thee; and thou shalt eat the herb of the field; [19] In the sweat of thy face shalt thou eat bread, **till thou return unto the ground; for out of it wast thou taken: for dust thou art, and unto dust shalt thou return**. [20] And Adam called his wife's name Eve; because she was the mother of all living. [21] Unto Adam also and to his wife did the LORD God make coats of skins, and clothed them. [22] And the LORD God said, **Behold, the man is become as one of us, to know good and evil: and now, lest he put forth his hand, and take also of the tree of life, and eat, and live for ever**. [23] Therefore the LORD God sent him forth from the garden of Eden, to till the ground from whence he was taken. [24] **So he drove out the man; and he placed at the east of the Garden of Eden Cherubim, and a flaming sword which turned every way, to keep the way of the tree of life**."

The Balancing Act

There are several things that we can derive from this passage of Scripture that relate directly to the sin nature. Most people never consider precisely what a sin nature 'is'. We talk about having it, but if you ask most church members to describe 'what it is', 'how it functions', and 'why it functions', few are capable of giving a valid answer.

Consider the following -   In the scene in the garden, shown above, the 'Fall' has already taken place. At what point does Adam possess the sin nature? Does the sin nature appear before the Fall? During the Fall? Or After the Fall? We must come to a conclusion pertaining to this point. We need to ascertain if our sin nature is related to free will in the first place. If sin is directly related to the free will choice that you and I make, it undermines the position of the Calvinists. Yet if free will is not related to sin, then we would be just as 'predestined to sin' as those who are 'predestined to salvation' would be. This would make God ungodly. ***<u>SO OUR SIN NATURE IS IRREVOCABLY CONNECTED WITH OUR FREE WILL</u>***.

Adam hides in the bushes as the Lord walks through the garden. What has really happened? Is Adam's nakedness caused by 'modesty' or by the truth that his sin (not his sin nature) is exposed? Is the awareness of sin equal to awareness of sin nature? Let's examine the question that God asks: "Who told you that you were naked?" Adam's response to the Lord is to shift blame from himself to Eve and, by implication, to the Lord Himself. Adam tries to explain his sin away by indicting Eve directly and God indirectly by inferring that his sin was caused by "That woman you gave me." His position is that **_IF GOD HAD NOT GIVEN HIM EVE, ADAM WOULD NEVER HAVE SINNED_**. This is not a Scriptural position and is indefensible under any circumstance. Adam had only two choices – to sin or to be obedient. The nature to sin must be linked to the issue of free will, for God had given him Eve only in the role as a 'helpmeet', not as a conscience. **_ALL MEN WANT TO HIDE THEIR SIN AND THEIR WEAKNESSES_**.

As Adam hides in the bushes and the Lord calls his name, is this simply to find Adam's location? Or does this imply something else entirely? We ascribe the trait of omniscience to the Lord, so we can eliminate the idea that God was trying to find Adam. God knew where he was, through His Divine power. Is the Lord aware that a man's sin nature requires that man try to hide his sin? You and I know that all sin and all unrighteousness offends God. Look at Psalm 51. David gives a remarkable testimony that God does not correct. Thus it must be true, as we read, "^{1}*To the chief Musician, A Psalm of David, when Nathan the prophet came unto him, after he had gone in to Bathsheba. Have mercy upon me, O God, according to thy lovingkindness: according unto the multitude of thy tender mercies blot out my transgressions. ^{2}Wash me thoroughly from mine iniquity, and cleanse me from my sin. ^{3}For I acknowledge my transgressions: and my sin is ever before me. ^{4}Against thee, thee only, have I sinned, and done this evil in thy sight: that thou mightest be justified when thou speakest, and be clear when thou judgest.*" This is David's confession after his committing adultery with Bathsheba (2 Samuel 11) is revealed by the prophet of the Lord, Nathan, over in 2

Samuel 12. David had committed adultery with Bathsheba and had sinned against both Bathsheba and Uriah (her husband) for making their marriage vows of no effect. He had placed Uriah in harm's way, so that he would be killed. He had conspired to keep the physical sin away from the people, except that Nathan confronts David with the truth. Yet when David offers this Psalm of repentance, he states that his sin was against God alone. God knew what David had done – there was no escaping that! But David's admission of the sin against God gives remarkable insight as to the depth of sin's offense. Just as it was in David's case, so was the sin in the garden. **ALL SIN OFFENDS GOD**. We need to be reminded of this fact each and every day! No matter how much we want to conceal sin, God always knows. That is why, over in Ecclesiastes 12:13-14, we see, "*^{13} Let us hear the conclusion of the whole matter: Fear God, and keep his commandments: for this is the whole duty of man. ^{14} For God shall bring every work into judgment, with every secret thing, whether it be good, or whether it be evil.*" **GOD KNOWS OF ALL SIN AND IF ALL SIN OFFENDS GOD, THE RESULT IS THAT THE SINS OF THE ELECT AND THE LOST OFFEND GOD EQUALLY**.

When confronted by the Lord, Adam doesn't answer the Lord's first question: Who told thee that thou wast naked? Why doesn't Adam tell the Lord the truth? The idea is that Adam and Eve were in innocence before sinning, but as a result of their sin, they exercised **self-judgment** in the realization that indeed their sin was exposed. **IF MAN WERE TO EXERCISE SELF-JUDGMENT BEFORE HE COMMITTED SIN, HE WOULD NOT HAVE CHOSEN TO SIN**.

Adam answers the questions of the Lord yet he tries to shift the blame from himself to Eve. What does this say about Adam's nature at this point? Here's a serious problem that every Christian must face. Is it easier to confess that we were wrong before our credibility is shot full of holes or after? This is the dilemma that all sinners face. Because we fail to exercise that self-judgment before we sin, we usually will do anything possible to conceal the sin. Adam's character is no better and no worse than the character that you and I exhibit. He tries to deflect God's wrath because he failed to exercise his own self-judgment. We are just as Adam. **_WE CHOOSE, THROUGH THE EXERCISE OF OUR FREE WILL, TO TRY TO CONCEAL OUR SIN FROM OTHER MEN AND WOMEN BECAUSE OF THE ISSUE OF PRIDE_**!

As the Lord pronounces judgment on the woman, He prescribes pain as part of the judgment. Is pain part of the sin nature? Many people would never consider 'pain' to be part of God's judgment or to be part of the sin nature. They only think of the pain associated with childbirth. Yet pain is inflicted each and every time we sin. There is no such thing, as the liberal lost would have you believe, as a victim-less crime. In every sin someone suffers. You can go down the list of sins, even to the issue of prostitution, and each sin carries pain to some degree. The pain may only be the issue of human dignity as the woman sells the use of her body, in equating true value as a commodity of the flesh. Or perhaps in the idea of a drug pusher - He is only giving people what they want; yet the drugs do something that prevents any man from being 'sober minded' as the Scripture commands. Man cannot come closer to God through the use of drugs, so the pain is there as man becomes frustrated at never finding God. But in each case, pain is the result of sin, not an integral part of the sin nature. Yet man chooses pain every day over the blessings of God, because man's sin nature is constantly prompting man to sin. **_PAIN IS THE RESULT OF SIN, NOT A PART OF THE HUMAN NATURE_**.

As the Lord introduces Adam to the concept of death, 'returning to dust', we must ask, 'Is the sin nature part of the Lord's judgment?' We know that before the Fall, Adam and Eve were to live eternally – as long as they lived in innocence. Once the covering of innocence was ripped away, man was fully exposed to sin. But that does not mean that the 'Sin Nature' of man was part of the Lord's judgment. Perhaps it would be better to ask why God chose to give man free will. Most people never consider the 'why' of the issue of free will. They only see the conflict that develops if they gravitate to one or the other positions relating to the free will issue.

Dr. Daniel F. Beckley

Chapter 8

More Conflict

Consider the implications of a world where there was no free will. Man could never make any choice that was not logical. Man would be seen as an automaton of some sort. In this condition, God, who calls men to worship, would not receive the voluntary response of man to worship his creator. Without the issue of free will, there can be neither true worship nor disobedience. It would be almost as if man were a robot, responding to certain stimuli and input, and, each time he was called to worship, man would respond in a mechanical sense only. There would be no giving from the heart. So where does the answer lie? We know that God loves a 'cheerful giver' (II Corinthians 9:7), one who exercises free will in giving back to the Lord out of love. God does not want the heartless worship of an automaton. He demands the worship of those who voluntarily seek Him and, in free choice, trust Him.

In creation, from Genesis 1:26-27, we discover a peculiarity about man's existence that demands that man have free will. Let's look at the passage, which says, " *²⁶ And God said,* **Let us make man in our image, after our likeness**: *and let them have dominion over the fish of the sea, and over the fowl of the air, and over the cattle, and over all the earth, and over every creeping thing that creepeth upon the earth.* ²⁷ **So God created man in his own image**, *in the image of God created he him; male and female created he them.*" The fact that we are created in the image of God demands that we have free will **_BEFORE THE FALL_**. The truth of this is found that Adam **_chose_** not to obey the Lord's command of not eating from the tree of knowledge of good and evil. The fact that Adam rebelled against what God had specifically forbid shows the free will choice in the act of sinning. Otherwise you suggest that the Lord had ordained that Adam would spend an eternity in the Lake of Fire. **_FREE WILL IS PART OF THE SIN PROCESS, NOT THE RESULT OF SIN_**.

Can the sin nature be reduced to the knowledge of good and evil, with the choice varying from time to time on the degree of lust? The answer to this question must be a resounding, "**No!**" The answer must be 'No', because God, Himself, possesses that same knowledge of good and evil. God's command that man not eat of the tree of knowledge of good and evil was not to prevent man from knowing the difference, but to prevent man from ruin. God's command was founded in love, while Satan's treachery was based on rebellion. His words to Eve, in Genesis 3:4, "*Ye shall not surely die,*" are rooted in deceit. God wished for man to live in innocence, while Satan wished for man to live in sin.

Look at the words of temptation that Satan used. In Genesis 3:5, he tells Eve, "*For God doth know that in the day ye eat thereof, then your eyes shall be opened, and ye shall be as gods, knowing good and evil.*" The resulting idea is that we could become as 'gods' - that we would be as God is, but also as the angels are. Satan was a member of the heavenly host. He knew the difference between good and evil. All angels knew the difference between good and evil. Yet that did not prevent many angels from choosing to sin against God. Being as God would require that we only consider the good, never even contemplating the evil that was possible. God chooses holiness and goodness exclusively. As a true definition, evil can be reduced to those things that the Lord will not entertain. **_KNOWLEDGE OF GOOD AND EVIL ALONE IS NOT SIN. FOR THAT KNOWLEDGE TO BECOME SIN REQUIRES THAT WE MERELY CONSIDER OR ULTIMATELY CHOOSE EVIL_**.

If God knew that the sin nature was to be carried by Adam (the X + Y Chromosome issue previously discussed), why did the Lord kick man out from the garden? Most certainly, it must be that God understood the disobedience of Adam was not going to be a one-time thing. As long as man existed in the garden in innocence, man was safe from harming himself. God had originally designed the garden for man to live within for all of eternity. But, as evidenced in man's failure to refrain from eating of the Tree of Knowledge of Good and Evil, man could not be trusted to refrain from eating of the Tree of Life.

As long as Adam lived, his sin would live with him. God could not let sin live forever. This was the Lord's reasoning in preventing Adam from ever eating of the Tree of Life. Once Adam had sinned and once Eve had sinned, God could not permit them to have access to eternal life – without full atonement for sin. That is the reason why Jesus had to die and why Adam and Eve lost the privilege of living forever in the garden. **_GOD COULD NOT TOLERATE SIN LIVING FOREVER_**.

But then why would God permit the sin nature to be passed on? Once man had the knowledge of choice, not simply the exercise of free will, man was doomed to have that sin nature. As long as man, through free will, knew that there was an alternative to obedience to God's commands, the sin nature would be passed on from generation to generation. ***SIN NATURE IS NOT GOD'S JUDGMENT OF MAN, BUT THE RESULT OF MAN'S FREE WILL EXERCISE OF CHOICE.***

Therefore, the Calvinistic viewpoint, as opposed to the Arminian viewpoint shown above, is more practical. The Calvinistic viewpoint on this topic is as follows - "**As a result of the Fall, man is totally depraved and dead in his sin; he is unable to save himself. Because he is dead in sin, God must initiate salvation.**"

Chapter 9

Premises & Promises

As we examine this viewpoint, it would appear that this statement of the Calvinist persuasion is more consistent with reality. Let's discuss the statement that we will consider as the starting point for "***The Third Option***."

As a result of the Fall, man is totally depraved and dead in his sin. This statement is absolutely true. While it is safe to say that there are depths of depravity, it is most assured that man, left by himself, will act in a depraved manner. If we consider the depths to which man would descend, outside of a right relationship with Jesus Christ, we can see the truth about this statement. In a country where over 90% say they believe in God, we also have a country where death is trivialized (abortion, euthanasia, and gang killings), life is minimized (triage in crisis situations, indifferent attitudes to the 'non-viable mass' in the abortion issue, drug addiction) and God is denied in our public schools. Imagine how much worse it would be if we lived in a society where God was forbidden or minimized.

Man is unable to save himself. Many churches love to sing the hymn '*Just As I Am*'. They love to sing it because it means that God accepts them exactly the way they are. Yet you will hear many of the less mature Christians say something like, "John has so much to offer God if he'd only come to Jesus." Unfortunately, this position does not stand up to God's Word. We accept Romans 3:23 at face value when we hear that "*all have sinned and have come short of the glory of God.*" Yet we never extend that verse to it's conclusion, as expressed in Isaiah 64:6, which tell us, "*But we are all as an unclean thing, and all our righteousnesses are as filthy rags; and we all do fade as a leaf; and our iniquities, like the wind, have taken us away.*" Who are we to assume that anything that we have to offer God has any value to Him if it is not purged of sin - all sin – and not just the ones we want to confess. We have absolutely nothing that God needs. We have nothing, except our lives given completely and freely, that God wants. Since we come short of the glory of God, what we have to offer God is like rags, the filthy wrappings that were used to cover the open wounds of lepers. Since nothing measures up, we have nothing to offer God and if nothing is worthy of Him, we cannot save ourselves.

Because man is spiritually dead through sin, God must initiate salvation. One of the most difficult things to realize is that, prior to salvation, man is spiritually dead to God. We do not possess life in any sense. We are dead men and women walking toward our graves, with our destiny in the lake of fire secure (John 3:16-21). We are dead, with absolutely no hope. Yet it is clear that God initiates salvation. Look at the book of Romans, Chapter 5. "[1] *Therefore being justified by faith, we have peace with God through our Lord Jesus Christ.* [2] *by whom also we have access by faith into this grace wherein we stand, and rejoice in hope of the glory of God.* [3] *And not only so, but we glory in tribulations also: knowing that tribulation worketh patience;* [4] *And patience, experience; and experience, hope:* [5] *And hope maketh not ashamed; because the* *love of God is shed abroad in our hearts by the Holy Ghost which is given unto us. ⁶ For when we were yet without strength, in due time Christ died for the ungodly. ⁷ For scarcely for a righteous man will one die: yet peradventure for a good man some would even dare to die. ⁸ But God commendeth his love toward us, in that, while we were yet sinners, Christ died for us. ⁹ Much more then, being now justified by his blood, we shall be saved from wrath through him. ¹⁰ For if, when we were enemies, we were reconciled to God by the death of his Son, much more, being reconciled, we shall be saved by his life. ¹¹And not only so, but we also joy in God through our Lord Jesus Christ, **by whom we have now received the atonement**. ¹²Wherefore, as by one man sin entered into the world, and death by sin; and so death passed upon all men, for that all have sinned: ¹³ (For until the law sin was in the world: but sin is not imputed when there is no law. ¹⁴ Nevertheless death reigned from Adam to Moses, even over them that had not sinned after the similitude of Adam's transgression, who is the figure of him that was to come)."* God had initiated His Divine plan of salvation even before Adam committed the first sin. That God came seeking fellowship with Adam, but was prevented by Adam's sin, cannot be denied. Therefore God knew of the only means of restoration even then. That is why we can say that God showed His love to you and me first, for Christ died before you or I even existed. His call to you and me from the cross at Calvary was the fulfillment of God's redemptive plan that was actually founded before Calvary ever had existed.

God did not impute sin to the entire human race through Adam's sin, but all people inherit a corrupt nature as a result of Adam's fall. Here is the second statement and if you look carefully, you find from the Moody table that it represents the Arminian point of doctrine. How does this statement balance with the Word of God? The first verse that should be examined is Romans 3:23, which says, "*For all have sinned and come short of the glory of God.*" Suffice it to say that without a sin nature, no one can sin. It is not possible to sin without that nature. Further study in the Word of God shows how complete the sin nature really is. Romans 3:10 tells us, "*As it is written, There is none righteous, no not one.*" This is a re-phrasing of Psalm 14:1 (*The fool hath said in his heart, there is no God. They are corrupt, they have done abominable works, and there is none that doeth good.*) and Psalm 14:3 (*They are all gone aside, they are all together become filthy: there is none that doeth good, no, not one*). Even if you consider the possibility that a man could be 'righteous in his own generation', such as Job is described, Job's righteousness pales in comparison to the Lord's. It will not stand the test for it still comes short of God's standard and God's glory, the Lord Jesus Christ. **THEREFORE SIN IS INDEED IMPUTED TO ALL MEN AND ALL MEN POSSESS THE SIN NATURE**.

Since we have rejected the Arminian position on this point, we need to consider the Calvinist's position on sin nature. Reading again from the table, we see the Calvinist's position stated as "**Through Adam's transgression, sin was imputed – passed to the entire race so that all people are born in sin**."

Does this statement balance with the Scripture quoted previously? **_THE SIN NATURE IN ALL MEN REQUIRES A SAVIOR FOR ALL MEN_**. Yes, it does.

God unconditionally, from eternity past, elected some to be saved. Election is not based on man's future response. This is one of the most illogical positions ever stated in a church's doctrine. I offer this comment without apology for Scripture never needs man to offer an apology. The statement and the position cannot balance with Scripture and it does not balance with the nature of God. Yet it is part of a dogmatic position that is central to Calvinist belief.

Consider the first part of the doctrinal statement. It establishes that God, from eternity past, ordained a list of people who would be overwhelmed with His call to salvation. It infers from the converse position that God therefore has ordained a list of people who would never respond to or even hear the Gospel call. It is an exclusionary doctrine that conflicts with and totally defies the doctrine of God's grace. It cannot be resolved with Scripture, for example 2 Peter 3:9b, which states that God is "*not willing that any should perish, but that all should come to repentance.*" It denies the purpose of the church, which has been commissioned to reach "every creature" with the Gospel message.

The latter part of this doctrinal statement denies man's ability to choose to accept God's call. It further denies man's participation in the choices which man must make, for man is a creature with curiosity and conviction. It eliminates the issue of free will, the choice to accept or reject all gifts, from heaven or earth. It denies man's unique standing of all of the creatures in God's creation, since man is the only specie with the affinity and the ability to acknowledge the Creator.

It does not stand the test of free will. For instance, if you tell a child not to touch the stove, what is the first thing that the child does? He, of course, touches the stove to see if you are telling the truth. Man's ability to grow is not a choice, but a requirement. It works in concert with curiosity in an ongoing quest for knowledge. **That striving for information is a free will choice. Whether man lives up to that choice, however, is another matter entirely**.

Chapter 10

Confusion & Complications

Now let's look at the opposing opinion from the Arminians. It states, "**God elected those whom He knew would believe of their own free will. Election is conditional, based on man's response in faith**." Although the position of the Arminians is closer to the truth, their doctrinal point is also flawed. When you are presented with divergent views on a point of doctrine, it does not mean that these are the only two possibilities that exist. In this case the latter part of the statement appears to be true, but there is error in the first part.

Consider the position that the latter part of the verse states. When we see the statement that 'Election is conditional, based on man's response in faith," we see the truth that the statement conveys. Men can be saved, but it is as they respond in faith to God's Call that salvation is attained. You and I exist in Christ within a faith covenant. Ephesians 2:8-10 tells us quite clearly, "*⁸ For by grace are ye saved through faith; and that not of yourselves: it is the gift of God: ⁹ Not of works, lest any man should boast. ¹⁰For we are his workmanship, created in Christ Jesus unto good works, which God hath before ordained that we should walk in them.*" You and I exist within that faith covenant, a covenant that requires maintenance on our part. It cannot be left to stand by idle, as it must produce results as evidence of the faith covenant. It proves your standing within Christ, standing as a joint-heir before the Father. It is the testimony of our transition from sinful man to the expressed image of Christ Jesus. That transition is stated most clearly within the passage of Romans 8:29, where we find, "**_For whom he did foreknow, he also did predestinate to be conformed to the image of his Son, that he might be the firstborn among many brethren_**."

This brings up the next issue: **WORDS MEAN THINGS, THUS DIFFERENT WORDS MEAN DIFFERENT THINGS**. Within the arena of ideas associated with modern theology, there are predisposed positions that are put forth each and every day. The predisposed positions, generally speaking, are given as support for an existing doctrinal practice. Such is the case where the words 'election', 'foreknowledge' and 'predestination' are used. In the Greek, examining the passage found in Romans 8:29, we see the following:

> Foreknow - 4267. proginosko, prog-in-oce'-ko; from G4253 and G1097; to know beforehand, i.e. foresee:--foreknow (ordain), know (before).
>
> Predestinate - 4309. proorizo, pro-or-id'-zo; from G4253 and G3724; to limit in advance, i.e. (fig.) predetermine:--determine before, ordain, predestinate.
>
> From the passage in Matthew 24:31, we have the word 'Elect' - 1588. eklektos, ek-lek-tos'; from G1586; select; by implication. favorite:--chosen, elect.

As you can plainly see, there are three different words and those three words that are translated in the KJV as Foreknow, Predestinate and Elect are from three different Greek words in a language with different meanings and implications. However, some attempt to use these words interchangeably, much to the confusion of the 'normal congregation member. Some Bible scholars sacrifice clarity of explanations if they do not fit into their own personal theology. The three words are, after my research, defined as follows:

Foreknowledge – This is a Divine term that can explain God's ability to see through the ages of eternity past and eternity future. To clearly see the truth of this statement, one must understand that the Lord exists outside of time. Time was given to man for convenience, in addition to constraint. Since the Lord transcends His creation, the constraints of this universe do not confine the Lord. From His perspective, outside of time, he has the ability to see the effects which changes produce His desired outcome. Since the Lord sees our lives in a kind of panorama, he 'fore-knows' what is best for us and what needs to be changed to produce the outcome of our being conformed to the image of Christ.

Predestinate – The easiest way to explain this term is to speak of God's Divine plan for the ages. The idea that man's **destiny** is determined by the Lord before all of the ages cannot be balanced with what we know about the nature of God from all of Scripture. Therefore we must acknowledge that **the Lord had a specific plan for those who would yield to His call to salvation**. When we respond to the Gospel call, God's 'predestinated' plan is for us to walk a sanctified life as is befitting someone who is a joint-heir of Jesus Christ. By choosing to walk according to God's plan, we can become more Christ-like, conforming more and more to the image of Jesus Christ, which is shown in glory by God's revealed Word.

Election – Election is the standing that each man holds as he hears the Gospel message. Election occurs when the hardness of our heart is shattered and then is to be sacrificed on the altar of our life. Yet it is not our own life that is ultimately sacrificed. Jesus Christ stands in our place as a guilty party, except that He hung on that cross some 2000 years ago. Election means that our life has been traded for the death of Jesus Christ. In that instant, we have our status changed from that of a lost man or lost woman to one of God's Redeemed, the elect of Christ.

So, if we look at Romans 8:29 again, we read, "*For whom he did foreknow* (**seen by God in a panorama through the ages**), *he also did predestinate* (**had a plan for them who are redeemed**) *to be conformed to the image of his Son, that he might be the firstborn among many brethren* (**the elect**)."

We have completed this exercise so that we will not attribute to God a characteristic that is childish or petty. We cannot ascribe to the Lord a character trait that even remotely casts aspersions on the nature of God. If we were to take the Arminian statement here, we give the Lord a characteristic that would more befit a selfish six-year old. To say that God looks down through time to see who has answered the salvation call and would call only those people would give God that precise characteristic. He would be guilty of having a temper tantrum at those who reject salvation and that would be ungodly behavior. We cannot allow this error to continue as doctrine.

One other point that needs to be discussed here relates to the idea of preaching the Gospel message. To preach and share the Gospel truth is one of the commands and privileges given specifically to the church by the Lord Jesus Christ. Under the Calvinist position of undeniable election, there is absolutely no need to preach the Gospel message. It would be ludicrous to imagine that God's call could possibly be influenced by any man's attempt to share the truth of the Gospel. Obviously, this position would not be in agreement with the Lord Jesus Christ's command that we preach the Gospel "*to every creature*" (Mark 16:15). Charles Spurgeon had one of the greatest ministries of all time. Preaching as many as eight sermons a day, Spurgeon was a Calvinist. Yet while he was a Calvinist who believed in limited election and limited atonement, he was also pragmatic. He believed his job was to preach the Gospel to the whole world. Unlike many other Calvinist preachers, who understand that their doctrinal position means that preaching the Gospel is not necessary, Spurgeon held a unique perspective on preaching. If he were to preach to everyone on the list of the 'Elect' and if all of those people had responded and were saved, then he believed it was God's job to elect some more. That posture indicates that Spurgeon had some degree of question about the Calvinist position of limited election.

Dr. Daniel F. Beckley

Clearly, neither the Calvinist nor the Arminian positions satisfy a firm doctrinal position. Neither is consistent with Scripture. Neither has the clear standing in comparison with God's Word. Thus a new statement, in full balance with the nature and character of God, in full agreement with the Word of God, must be developed.

Chapter 11

God to the Rescue

"**God determined that Christ would die for all those whom God elected. Since Christ did not die for everyone, but only for those who were elected to be saved, His death is completely successful**."

The position promoted here is called the limited atonement posture. It is a Calvinist position and it implies once again that God has a limited concept of salvation. Aside from the positions presented in point 3, doesn't the idea of God, mixed with anything in a limited fashion, present us with an oxymoron? God cannot be limited in any of His functions as long as they do not conflict with His Divine nature.

If you were willing to examine any of the Lord's characteristics, which of them can be limited? God is the absolute perfection of all that is good. There are certain attributes that are God's alone, yet man struggles daily to achieve even a glimmer of those traits. The table below will provide a contrast for you to consider about man's goals and God's nature.

Man Strives To Be	God Already Is
Faithful	Faith
Hopeful	Hope
Merciful	Mercy
Kind	Kindness
Charitable	Charity
Loving	Love
Holy	Holiness
Righteous	Righteousness
Gracious	Grace
Knowledgeable	Knowledge
Wise	Wisdom
Peaceful	Peace
Honorable	Honor
Content	Contentment
Truthful	Truth
Consistent	Consistency

Although you and I strive to achieve great things, we still come short of the glory of God. In falling short of the goal, we fail in every category. We fall short because of the perfection that we find in the Lord's character. If there are no shortcomings in the Lord's character, then there can be no shortcomings in His execution of the Divine plan of redemption.

Let's look at the Arminian viewpoint. It says, "**Christ died for the entire human race, making all mankind savable. His death is effective only in those who believe.**" Does this balance with what we know of God and His nature? The answer in this case is a resounding "**Yes!**" The first part of the statement balances with Scripture (II Peter 3:9 – "*not willing*

that any should perish, but that all should come to repentance.") and with God's nature (Loving and Merciful).

Think of the shedding of blood by Jesus as a series of checks drawn on a heavenly bank account. Each member of the human race is given a check in the amount of $ 100,000,000 (One Hundred Million Dollars – representing the opportunity of salvation). In order for the checks to have any value, they must be cashed (the means of gaining the benefit – in this case receiving eternal life in salvation by grace through faith). If the checks are never cashed, never redeemed, they are of no value to the person to whom the check was given. But the price paid for the check is not diminished in any sense because the check has been made ineffective (not redeemed). The funds are available (the price has been paid), but the choice to cash the check and redeem the check for the amount of money it represents remains not with the person who issues the check, but with the person who has received the check.

A person who does not accept salvation as a free gift does not diminish the sacrifice of Christ. Christ died for all who would accept the free gift of salvation. The recipient, as stated in Ephesians 2, can never diminish the gift. The gift is always valued on the intent of the giver.

Common grace is extended to all mankind but is insufficient to save anyone. Through irresistible grace God drew to Himself those whom He had elected, making them willing to respond. The ideal of grace has been in dispute for almost as long as Calvinism and Arminianism have been debated. Calvinists and Arminians hold differing views of grace. Covenant theologians hold differing opinions from those promoted by Dispensational theologians. Debate over the differences between 'common grace' and 'saving grace' are passionate. Others, such as those of the Catholic Church, believe that the church is the exclusive channel of grace – flowing from the throne of God through the conduit of the faithful church.

Perhaps we need to define what 'grace' really is. We should also state categorically what it is not, in relationship with various denominational postures. Some define grace as 'God's unmerited favor' and in a narrow sense that is correct. A more complete definition would be the acrostic that shows grace as '***God's Riches At Christ's Expense***.'

Chapter 12

Confusing Catechisms

Some would suggest that the idea of grace is unmerited favor, while others prefer to posit that there are 'degrees' of grace and that they, as the only recognized church body, are the exclusive dispensers of that grace. This position is doctrinal in the Roman Catholic Church. In the book *The Catholic Catechism*, by John A. Hardon, S.J., in chapter 6, The Grace of God, Hardon writes:

> "Among the mysteries of the Catholicism, none is more practically important for our personal and social lives than the doctrine of grace. It is the very heart of Christianity on its human side, since it describes the panorama of God's dealings with each one of us in the depths of our souls. The study of grace corresponds in theology to the science of psychology, but with implications in every aspect of the Christian religion that have no counterpart in merely human philosophy."

> "All the dogmas of faith take on new meaning from the existence of a supernatural order. The Trinity of persons is meaningful because their eternal communication within the Deity are the source of his gifts outside the divinity. They are the fountainhead of grace from the Father, through his Son, our Lord, in the Spirit who dwells in the souls of the justified."

> "By the very fact that we believe in things unseen and hope for the promised reward of those who love God, we are witnesses to the action of a superhuman power, which is divine grace operating on the mind and will and enabling us to see and want that the natural man cannot perceive or desire."
>
> "We say that the sacraments are seven signs instituted by Christ to confer the grace they signify. And more broadly we hold that the Catholic Church is the great sacrament of the New Law that Christ founded to be the unique channel of grace to all mankind, with special title to those who are baptized and active members of the Mystical Body of Christ. But no matter how conceived, the sacraments are so far significant and membership in the Church so much more appreciated if we see the great mysteries of Christ in their true perspective as visible and human agencies for the transmission of invisible divine blessings to the human race."

I have introduced the first four paragraphs of the sixth chapter of the book written by the Reverend Hardon so that you may see how the idea of grace has been pushed and pulled to serve one denomination's purposes. For instance, the idea that God's grace is available exclusively through the Catholic Church is a means of keeping the "faithful" firmly held in place by 'mysteries'. God's grace is no mystery! God's grace is the wonderful outpouring from the heavenly throne to the believer exclusively because of the believer's stand **_in faith, in Christ_**, not simply because they were baptized as a child into a church and attend services twice each year. As shown in Acts Chapter 8, there is no real baptism outside of one which is accompanied by true belief in Christ as the exclusive atonement for man's sins.

While grace is God's gift to mankind, there can be no varying degrees of grace. In Paul's trial due to his thorn in the flesh, he had prayed three times for the Lord to remove the infirmity, yet God instructed Paul to bear the infirmity simply because God's grace is "*sufficient for thee*" (II Corinthians 12:9). God's grace is sufficient for the moment to each and every believer. The idea that you have a different 'type' of grace for each circumstance that a believer encounters is, at a minimum, a stretch. **Jesus revealed the 'mysteries'** to the disciples, thus given also to the church. In John 15:14-15, we see, "*[14]Ye are my friends, if ye do whatsoever I command you. [15]Henceforth I call you not servants; for the servant knoweth not what his lord doeth: but I have called you friends; for all things that I have heard of my Father I have made known unto you.*" Jesus hasn't wrapped Christianity in superstition, He has revealed the truth to His friends. The only way to be one of Jesus' friends is to have that **unique personal relationship that comes exclusively through salvation by grace through faith, not via infant baptism or by participation in social or religious activities at a church**.

There are several types of 'grace' that various groups use to describe the God's gift. Some refer to **common grace**, which seems to be a general type of grace that is poured out freely and without measure on all of mankind. Others believe there is **prevenient grace**, which seems to be used as a precursor to the grace needed for salvation. Then there are others who believe in **saving grace**, which is used as a tool by the Holy Spirit in true salvation experiences, to overwhelm man so he will accept, and not reject, salvation (Calvinists call this **irresistible grace**). Those who embrace 'Covenant Theology' believe that, today, we live under a covenant of grace. 'Dispensationalists' believe that God's grace has been poured out in varying measure, according to the need of man in each 'dispensation'. It is difficult at best to discern which groups embrace which ideal, although a literal Scriptural view is that God's grace is liberally given to His children.

In a purely free will condition, man may choose to accept or reject the grace of God. We act, on occasion, as petulant children. We refuse to accept the things from God that are good for us and we would rather accept something else that is counterfeit and corrupt. In Matthew 7 (with parallel passage in Luke 11), we find the truth about God's character and see how he deals with His children. "[7]*Ask, and it shall be given you; seek, and ye shall find; knock, and it shall be opened unto you*: [8] *For every one that asketh receiveth; and he that seeketh findeth; and to him that knocketh it shall be opened.* [9] *Or what man is there of you, whom if his son ask bread, will he give him a stone?* [10] *Or if he ask a fish, will he give him a serpent?* [11] *If ye then, being evil, know how to give good gifts unto your children, how much more shall your Father which is in heaven give good things to them that ask him?*" God gives things to you and me although we do not seek them in a righteous sense. We want the things that please us.

The Balancing Act

As God gives us things in response to prayer, the Lord goes above and beyond the things we need by giving us unmerited grace.

Let's look at what the Arminians have to say. "**Through prevenient or preparatory grace, which is given to all people, man is able to cooperate with God and respond to Him in salvation. Prevenient grace reverses the effects of Adam's sin**." Does this sound any more reasonable than the Calvinist viewpoint? Hardly!

I believe that many people confuse the working of the Holy Spirit with the concept of grace. It isn't just grace that opens the door for man to receive salvation. God, through the office of the Holy Spirit, works on the heart of man as he hears the Gospel message. It is not mere grace at this moment in people's lives, it is the personal involvement of the Creator of this universe who has seen fit to personally and privately work on the hardness of your heart which then enables you to respond.

The second issue that fails the test of balancing the Arminian statement with Scripture is the idea that any kind of grace can change or overrule the nature of man, which would be necessary if we were to reverse the effects of Adam's sin. God cannot and, more importantly, will not overrule any trait, characteristic, trend or delegated authority that man possesses. If God would and could operate in this manner, it would have been easier for the Lord to simply terminate the lives of Adam and Eve in the garden. However, the Lord, in Genesis 1:28, had given man dominion over the earth and all of the inhabitants of the earth. Since God had given man a free gift – dominion over the earth - God would not transgress on that delegated authority. He could not, would not, be an 'Indian giver'. He could not simply take back or change the rules about that which He had clearly and completely delegated the authority.

Depravity extends to all of man, including his will. Without irresistible grace man's will remains bound, unable to respond to God on its own ability. The first segment of the statement, that "depravity extends to all of man, including his will", would seem to be valid. By observing a small child that comes from the womb crying, shrieking and in violent protest, we see an example of the selfish nature of humans. As the child grows older, no one has to teach the child to be greedy or to lie. It is human nature that causes the child acts in such a manner. I can recall my daughter, Sarah, at age 3, as she sat there with Oreo cookie crumbs smeared all over her face, telling me she had not eaten a cookie. While this does not categorically prove the depravity of man, it does testify to the subtle depths to which it does extend.

Consider the idea to which 'character' can be reduced. The greatest indication of the character of any one individual is that which a person does when no one else is around. For some, it is the escape from reality that is found in reading a book. For others, it is the escape from reality that is found in spending time in a bar or beer-joint, looking for adventure with a person of the opposite (or possibly the same) sex. The depth of depravity is staggering when you consider the number of people, from Christian and secular society, who have been found to lead a 'double life'. Suffice it to say that depravity is evidenced by the horrific crimes that men and women commit against each other. Murder is the theft of a life, placing no value on life itself except in the thrill of seeing another human being plead for their life while it is being extinguished. Adultery is the theft of intimacy and fidelity from a marriage, justified by others as a victimless crime where people choose to seek self-fulfillment. Pornography is another circumstance that secular humanists suggest is a victimless crime, yet it steals a basic human dignity from men and women who engage in all aspects of the 'industry'. Far greater perversion is shown when it extends to children, who are robbed of their childhood and subjected to acts that their immature minds have no ability to comprehend. Contrary to the opinion of most Americans and certainly the NAACP, slavery still exists today, stealing the basic freedoms that are taken for granted in this country today. Slavery involves those who are white, black, oriental, and every race on God's green earth. Like it or not, we can say with a surety that man is a depraved creature.

We must examine the idea of how God's grace can be 'irresistible' for some, but not for all. The basic premise negates the viability of the position, since that premise challenges the omnipotence of God. How can we even begin to undermine the character of God? How dare we place limits on the abilities of God! I would suggest that any reader who promotes that God is limited in the effective nature of His grace, without man's participation, read the 38th Chapter of the Book of Job.

In that passage, Job is confronted with the reality of man's distinctly inferior position, which should preclude man from issuing any challenge to the Lord. If we issue such a challenge, we would be operating on such an arrogant and flawed platform, our very souls would be in jeopardy of judgment and eternal damnation to the lake of fire. I will address the issue of God's sovereignty in the 7th point and the perseverance of the saints in the 8th point of doctrine.

Let's examine the Arminian position on this point. The Arminian position states, "**Prevenient grace is given to all people and exercised on the entire person, giving man a free will**." Aside from the issue of prevenient grace, which I believe to be a flawed doctrine; the phrase 'free will choice' could be better used in this instance. Perhaps the greatest gift that God has ever given to man, aside from the gift of eternal life through the blood of Jesus Christ, is the ability for each man, woman and child to have the choice of going to hell. Free will is not a concept that God gave man without great thought. Consider how much like Pavlov's dog man would be were free will not given by God to us. Those of us whom God had called would be sitting there, just like Mr. Pavlov's puppy, awaiting the external stimuli to which we would respond in the salvation experience. There would be no means for us to delay the response. There would be no rejection and, more importantly, no consideration of what God had done for us if free will is not the means of choice. If man cannot consider the price that God paid, then man cannot possibly show true gratitude or thanksgiving for God's grace. What would be the point of saving man if thanks cannot be given, except as a mute trophy of what God can do when He puts the Divine mind to it? God cannot get the glory in the circumstance where a man, in response to a proscribed set of terms and stimuli, reacts as an automaton. Yet this is exactly what a Calvinist doctrine promotes and yet the Arminian position of 'prevenient grace' is more of a convenience than a real doctrine that honors God. If, in any step of salvation or a redeemed man's actions, God does not get the glory, it cannot be anything that has originated from the throne of God. Again, we will discuss this item during the 7th point.

Dr. Daniel F. Beckley

Chapter 13

God is in Control

God limits His control in accord with man's freedom and response. His decrees are related to foreknowledge of what man's response will be. Thus is the Arminian statement about the sovereignty of God. That God limits his action based upon the free will submission of man to the Divine Plan of God and the Divine Will of God is absolutely correct. Consider a man who answers an advertisement by a church for service as a youth pastor. It cannot be argued from any point that the Divine Will of God desires anything other than our availability for service on behalf of Christ and His kingdom. But what if the man's response is not in direct response to a call from the Lord? Can the man, in this instance, be working in compliance with the Divine Plan of God? God, who also has free will and exercises it with each and every action, can choose to let the man continue or cause some event which will prevent the man from serving in that capacity. The fact that God can limit His control verifies that He has free will and, in that man is made in God's image, man also possesses the gift of free will. When the Lord said, in Genesis 1:26, "*Let us make man in our image, after our likeness,*" He was choosing (exercising free will) to make man possess the same free will that the Lord has.

The Calvinist point of view is as follows, "**God's sovereignty is absolute and unconditional. He has determined all things according to the good**

pleasure of His will. His foreknowledge originates in advanced planning, not in advanced information." The Calvinist viewpoint begins with the phrase, "God's sovereignty is absolute and unconditional." This is not correct. God's sovereignty is absolute but conditional and dependent on man's free will response. This condition will continue to exist until Christ returns and places all under His foot.

Perhaps we might use the explanation that **man's free will is temporal, while God's sovereignty is eternal**. I present to you two examples with corresponding Scripture of the balance between God's sovereignty and man's free will:

Consider the churches of Macedonia, of whom Paul speaks of over in 2nd Corinthians 8:1-6. "*Moreover, brethren, we do you to wit of the grace of God bestowed on the churches of Macedonia; How that in a great trial of affliction the abundance of their joy and their deep poverty abounded unto the riches of their liberality. For to their power, I bear record, yea, and beyond their power they were willing of themselves; Praying us with much intreaty that we would receive the gift, and take upon us the fellowship of the ministering to the saints. And this they did, not as we hoped, but first gave their own selves to the Lord, and unto us by the will of God. Insomuch that we desired Titus, that as he had begun, so he would also finish in you the same grace also.*" These churches subjected their free will to the sovereignty of God as part and parcel of their faith covenant with the Lord — voluntarily, in this temporal existence as well as in eternity.

The Balancing Act

Consider a rebellious man, who has rejected God for all of his life. After his death, he is doomed to an eternity in the lake of fire. This is his just reward for exercising his free will choice during his lifetime – rejecting Christ's atonement for his sins. This is temporal exercise of his free will. However, there is a step that will occur between his death and his final destination, described in Romans 14:11. Philippians 2:9-11 gives a more detailed account. There we read, "*Wherefore God also hath highly exalted him, and given him a name which is above every name: That at the name of Jesus every knee should bow, of things in heaven, and things in earth, and things under the earth; And that every tongue should confess that Jesus Christ is Lord, to the glory of God the Father.*" As the passage clearly states, this man's knee will bow before the Sovereign of this universe. God's exercise of His sovereignty is at His discretion. There is no conflict between God's sovereignty and man's free will because God is sovereign whether we say so – or not. Our opinion doesn't change a thing.

Next, we need to consider how 'determined' things really are. Some refute the position taken by the Calvinists as being nothing more than horoscopes and implementing zodiac fates. Keep in mind that God expects man to live a sanctified life, yet, as Paul points out again and again in his epistles, there is a constant war between the flesh and the spirit. Is this, too, ordained by God? 1st Corinthians 7:15 states that "*God hath called us to peace.*" This would seem to contradict the idea that the war between the flesh and the spirit is unnatural. But when we look at the truth of Scripture, with specific emphasis on the book of Romans, we see that we have peace with God, not with our flesh (Romans 5:1). The problem is that my life and the life of every other Christian is a constant struggle between the flesh and the spirit. Paul states in Romans 7 the problem clearly and concisely – it is a constant struggle for a man, even an apostle, such as Paul.

Romans 7 "*[7] What shall we say then? is the law sin? God forbid. Nay, I had not known sin, but by the law: for I had not known lust, except the law had said, Thou shalt not covet. [8] But sin, taking occasion by the commandment, wrought in me all manner of concupiscence. For without the law sin was dead. [9] For I was alive without the law once: but when the commandment came, sin revived, and I died. [10] And the commandment, which was ordained to life, I found to be unto death. [11] For sin, taking occasion by the commandment, deceived me, and by it slew me. [12] Wherefore the law is holy, and the commandment holy, and just, and good. [13] Was then that which is good made death unto me? God forbid. But sin, that it might appear sin, working death in me by that which is good; that sin by the commandment might become exceeding sinful. [14] For we know that the law is spiritual: but I am carnal, sold under sin. [15] For that which I do I allow not: for what I would, that do I not; but what I hate, that do I. [16] If then I do that which I would not, I consent unto the law that it is good. [17] Now then it is no more I that do it, but sin that dwelleth in me. [18] For I know that in me (that is, in my flesh,) dwelleth no good thing: for to will is present with me; but how to perform that which is good I find not. [19] For the good that I would I do not: but the evil which I would not, that I do.* ²⁰ *Now if I do that I would not, it is no more I that do it, but sin that dwelleth in me.* ²¹ *I find then a law, that, when I would do good, evil is present with me.* ²² *For I delight in the law of God after the inward man:* ²³ *But I see another law in my members,* **warring against the law of my mind, and bringing me into captivity to the law of sin which is in my members.** ²⁴ *O wretched man that I am! who shall deliver me from the body of this death?* ²⁵ *I thank God through Jesus Christ our Lord. So then with the mind I myself serve the law of God; but with the flesh the law of sin."*

Let me point out that this passage from Romans 7 isn't just preacher talk. Paul speaks, from first hand experience, about the war between the flesh and the spirit. That is why over in Galatians 5:16-18, Paul speaks with authority when he states, "¹⁶ *This I say then,* **Walk in the Spirit, and ye shall not fulfil the lust of the flesh.** ¹⁷ *For the flesh lusteth against the Spirit, and the Spirit against the flesh: and these are contrary the one to the other: so that ye cannot do the things that ye would.* ¹⁸ *But if ye be led of the Spirit, ye are not under the law."* If the Spirit leads us, we then are available to be used by God and to participate, at His calling under His sovereignty, in the Divine Plan by the Divine Will.

Jesus is the ultimate example of being led by the spirit of God. He existed on this earth as the hypostatic union – all God and all Man but at the same time. There is the issue which questions whether Jesus Christ could have sinned. Consider that His human side was subject to Temptation (see Matthew 4 and Luke 4), but because He is the ultimate example of following the leading of the Spirit, His Divine side would not, could not, sin.

Believers will persevere in the faith. Believers are secure in their salvation; none will be lost. This is the heart of controversy between those of the Calvinist or the Arminian persuasion. The Calvinists hold tightly to the issue of **perseverance** because of the sovereignty of God while Arminians cling to the free will choice of losing salvation because of the faults within man. The Arminian position is stated as "**Believers may turn from grace and lose salvation.**"

So, from these two diverse opinions, what can possibly be the point of intersection at the top of the Gateway Arch? Perhaps an examination of the attributes of God and the character of man would be beneficial because there is no rational way of placing the two statements into harmony. Or have we not studied Scripture at such a great level to become aware of God's truth?

Chapter 14

The Third Option

After all of the words and all of the rationalizing that we have done to this point, we have not yet established that there is a valid third position available to us. Yet all study of Scripture is beneficial to mankind because it gives us a greater knowledge of a God who loved mankind so much as to offer Himself as the sacrifice. This is the reason why a third option is necessary. Since God offered Himself, in the person of Jesus Christ, on the cross to restore mankind, is it not reasonable that we should seek everything that can be known about the loving God with whom we shall spend eternity?

As we examine this potential solution to the question of the Gateway Arch's point of intersection, also known as the dispute between Calvinists and Arminians, let me be frank about one very important point. This is only a potential solution. I am not foolish enough to suggest that this is the only correct position, nor am I dogmatic enough to say that no further searching of God's Word is needed. Quite the opposite, I believe that all men and women who read this presentation should continue their search of God's Word. They should study the Greek, Hebrew and Aramaic words. They should discuss the phrases used in a specific passage, with the context noted and the points of who, what, where, when, how and why observed and properly stored. They should debate the merit of the **Third Option** with the positions of the Calvinists and Arminians well represented, but only for the purpose of finding the

Lord's truth. As we prepare for the Lord's imminent return, let us be found faithful stewards of God's Word, specifically for the glory and honor of our Lord Jesus Christ.

Let's discuss the issue of covenants. When Jesus Christ instituted the ordinance of the Lord's Supper, reading from the Gospel of John, the Lord said that this involved the "blood of the new testament." Jesus Christ, as stated clearly in the Book of Hebrews, fulfilled the old testament and established a new testament, a new and better covenant for you and me.

In examining Scripture, the first use of the word 'covenant' occurs in Genesis 6:18. It involves the Lord establishing a covenant with Noah but it is a covenant that is dependant on one thing and one thing alone – **obedience**. Noah had a free will choice to make – obey or disobey. If he were disobedient, then Noah and his family would have perished. If he were obedient, then Noah and his family would be 'saved'. All of this occurs because, as Genesis 6:8 shows, "*Noah found **grace** in the eyes of the Lord.*" God's grace occurs **before obedience within the covenant**. God establishes the covenant of obedience because Noah has been found faithful previously, although the details are not specifically listed in Scripture.

The word that is translated as 'covenant' is the Hebrew word 'beriyth'. The word is specifically listed in Strong's exhaustive concordance as Hebrew Word 1285. The pronunciation of the word 'beriyth', is ber-eeth'. The root word means to cut or to establish. When a covenant is established, such as a peace treaty, the success of the treaty or covenant is always based on obedience to the covenant. To what purpose would people sign a contract, a covenant or a testament if they had no intention of being obedient to the requirements of the covenant?

Later when the Abrahamic covenant is established, God required a sign of obedience. That sign was not compliance with the Mosaic Law or any other Jewish ritual, except for circumcision, the cutting of the male foreskin. Obedience is always required of man when God establishes a covenant. Note that in this case it is a blood signature to the covenant, a case that also applies to the Cross and the Ultimate Sacrifice.

As we go through the covenants that were established involving Isaac, Jacob, Moses and David, again there is an expectation of obedience to the terms of the covenant. On one side of the covenant, there is the Lord, faithful and true in every thing that He does. He fulfills every contract above and beyond the requirements of the covenant each and every time. Unfortunately, man has not always been found faithful to the terms of the covenants. It seems that man's rebellious nature, also known as the depraved nature, shows up in each covenant and obedience fades as time goes by. In the case of Moses, after he went up Mount Sinai to receive the Ten Commandments, written by the finger of God, we find the children of Israel gathering precious metals and precious stones to make gods to worship. The rebellious children had disobeyed the first, second and third commandments that had been so recently given to them. While God is faithful to covenants, man is not.

Consider Jesus' own words, which are used by those who seek to show security in salvation, as He spoke in prayer to the Father. We find in John 17:12, "*While I was with them in the world,* **_I kept them in thy name: those that thou gavest me I have kept, and none of them is lost_**, *but the son of perdition; that the scripture might be fulfilled.*" When Jesus spoke these words, Judas Iscariot had already committed his act of betrayal. He, of course, is considered the son of perdition referred to by Jesus. The question that must be considered is whether this verse can be extended to Christians through the ages. Unfortunately, no answer is valid without other support from Scripture, which is silent.

If we are going to look at the words of Jesus, let's examine several passages:

The Parable of the Sower and the Seed – (Matthew 13). *[1] The same day went Jesus out of the house, and sat by the sea side. [2] And great multitudes were gathered together unto him, so that he went into a ship, and sat; and the whole multitude stood on the shore. [3] And he spake many things unto them in parables, saying, Behold, a sower went forth to sow; [4] And when he sowed, some seeds fell by the way side, and the fowls came and devoured them up: [5] Some fell upon stony places, where they had not much earth: and forthwith they sprung up, because they had no deepness of earth: [6] And when the sun was up, they were scorched; and because they had no root, they withered away. [7] And some fell among thorns; and the thorns sprung up, and choked them: [8] But other fell* *into good ground, and brought forth fruit, some an hundredfold, some sixtyfold, some thirtyfold. ⁹Who hath ears to hear, let him hear."*

In this passage, Jesus gives us great insight as to how people become 'saved'. Salvation must be found through the Word of God ... except in the case of those in distant lands who have never heard the Gospel message. It is true that, as Romans 10:17 tells us, *"So then faith cometh by hearing, and hearing by the word of God."* As Jesus delivers this parable of the sower and the seed, the first in a series of seven parables, the disciples question why he speaks in parables. Jesus, in verses 11-13, gives a remarkable answer, which some believe that it gives validity to an idea of limited atonement. He tells them, *"¹¹ He answered and said unto them, Because it is given unto you to know the mysteries of the kingdom of heaven, but to them it is not given. ¹² For whosoever hath, to him shall be given, and he shall have more abundance: but whosoever hath not, from him shall be taken away even that he hath. ¹³ Therefore speak I to them in parables: because they seeing see not; and hearing they hear not, neither do they understand."* In this instance, however, Jesus is not speaking of limited atonement in a New Testament sense. He was speaking of His mission to come to the house of Israel first and then, if rejected, to the gentile nations. That is why Paul says three times, in Romans 1:16, 2:9 and 2:10, to the Jew first and then to the gentiles.

Jesus then goes on to explain the passage Himself. We find this beginning in verse 18 of Matthew 13. Jesus says, *"¹⁸ Hear ye therefore the parable of the sower. ¹⁹*

When any one heareth the word of the kingdom, and understandeth it not, then cometh the wicked one, and catcheth away that which was sown in his heart. This is he which received seed by the way side. [20] *But he that received the seed into stony places, the same is he that heareth the word, and anon with joy receiveth it;* [21] *Yet hath he not root in himself, but dureth for a while: for when tribulation or persecution ariseth because of the word, by and by he is offended.* [22] *He also that received seed among the thorns is he that heareth the word; and the care of this world, and the deceitfulness of riches, choke the word, and he becometh unfruitful.* [23] *But he that received seed into the good ground is he that heareth the word, and understandeth it; which also beareth fruit, and bringeth forth, some an hundredfold, some sixty, some thirty."*

Here is the explanation. There are four places where the Word of God, the seed, lands. The first is the wayside or cart path, the second is among the stones, the third among the thorns and finally the fourth is among good and fertile soil.

The wayside or cart path: Since this is not a place where you wanted the seed to land in the first place, there is no expectation that the seed will have an opportunity to bear fruit. Immediately after the sower passes, the seed is 'stolen' by birds. The birds, in this instance, represent the demons and minions of Satan, whose efforts are to steal the Word of God from the hearts of man. Some interpret this as another example of limited atonement, where there are those who are not supposed to hear the Gospel call. I do not believe this to be an accurate assessment. It appears to me that there are always bystanders who are observing Christians in action. These people usually are quite worldly and have no interest in hearing the Word of God. Many within this group are offended when they see the '700 Club' or some other Christian program on TV or who complain loudly when Christian radio is in the place of the 'elevator music'. They have already made a conscious decision that Jesus Christ has no place in their world – but that does not mean that Christ does not want them to come to repentance. They suffer from a hardened heart, just like Pharaoh. Every time God's hand is revealed to them they reject it outright because of the hardness of their heart.

The stony ground: Here is a person that is clearly supposed to hear the Word of God. They hear the Word of God and respond in a free will choice to say **they want the gift of God** – salvation. Yet there is a problem, a crisis, that exists in the life of this individual – something as minor as cigarette smoking or perhaps something serious as physical abuse of a spouse. If they do nothing about the problem, they will wither away and their faith will die. In this case, there is no firm foundation on which to stand. There is no place for the deep roots to grow. The rocks and stones impede fruitful growth. And when that trial or tribulation comes to be common knowledge – not if, but when it comes – he has no sure foundation upon which he can stand. John 15:5 tells of the ultimate result, *"If a man abide not in me, he is cast forth as a branch, and is withered; and men gather them, and cast them into the fire, and they are burned."* **Did they lose salvation or did they never have it**?

The thorny ground. This person also is supposed to hear the word of God and like the one whose life is on the stony ground, this one also responds to the Gospel message. This one also faces the possibility that their faith will die away also. This possibility, like the one on the stony ground, is the concern of the debate on security in salvation or free will choice to turn away from salvation. He is overwhelmed by the cares of this world. He is consumed by worldly wealth and blinded by worldly possessions. The things of this world choke this individual! In Luke 18, we see the result of someone who wanted 'eternal life' but was unwilling to loose the 'things of this world'. Luke 18:22-25 tells us, " *[22] Now when Jesus heard these things, he said unto him, Yet lackest thou one thing: sell all that thou hast, and distribute unto the poor, and thou shalt have treasure in heaven: and come, follow me. [23] And when he heard this, he was very sorrowful: for he was very rich. [24] And when Jesus saw that he was very sorrowful, he said, how hardly shall they that have riches enter into the kingdom of God! [25] For it is easier for a camel to go through a needle's eye, than for a rich man to enter into the kingdom of God.*" The disciples who observed this encounter then asked Jesus, "*Who then can be saved?*" As the young man **walks away from the opportunity at eternal life**, did he ever truly complete the transaction? **Was he ever saved?**

The fertile ground. This is the case where the soil has all impediments removed. The process of removing those impediments is long or short, truly dependent on your commitment to the Lord and your constant working through the process on a daily basis. The stones are removed and the thorns are pulled up and burned. The Word of God can take effect in this place and bring forth fruit. Not only will it bring forth fruit, it bears much fruit – thirty times, sixty times, or even one hundred times fruit. From John 15, we know that bearing fruit comes from ***abiding in the true vine, Jesus Christ***. That abiding is certainly not a momentary event! It requires and it demands that we have a ***permanent dwelling WITHIN the vine***. We draw all things necessary for growth from the source, the vine in which we abide. If we fail to abide where we belong, we cannot grow. If we do not abide, can we expect to bear fruit? Can we possibly be mistaken for being part of the vine?

Now I will be the first to admit that I am not a farmer, but there is certain logic to farming that surpasses the occupation. I may not be able to say just when is the right time to plant. I may not be able to decide whether peas or cucumbers should be planted in which type of soil. But I ***know*** that ***if I prepare the ground, removing weed and stone from the land where I plant, there is a result that far exceeds the original sowing***. Pulling out weeds and thorns is hard work. Removing stones and rocks from the ground is quite a heavy task. But there is a benefit realized if we perform the task.

When I finally surrendered to the Lord in 1984, I was going through one of the most difficult times in my life. But as I grew, in Christ, nurtured by the Word of God, I saw that ***I needed to do the gardening***. It was something that I was required to do. I would see the benefit if I performed the task. But what happens if I

Dr. Daniel F. Beckley

do not put the required effort into my spiritual life? This is the question that must be answered.

Chapter 15

The Balancing Act

The problem that we face is that we so desperately want to have security in salvation, but we don't want the responsibility for the maintenance and upkeep of our eternal destiny. The problem is that the Word of God says that God is faithful ... man is not. God can change all things and make them new ... man cannot. So where is the balance? Let's examine the faithfulness of God.

Being confident of this very thing - Philippians 1. "³ I thank my God upon every remembrance of you, ⁴ Always in every prayer of mine for you all making request with joy, ⁵ For your fellowship in the gospel from the first day until now; ⁶ **Being confident of this very thing, that he which hath begun a good work in you will perform it until the day of Jesus Christ**: ⁷ Even as it is meet for me to think this of you all, because I have you in my heart; inasmuch as both in my bonds, and in the defence and confirmation of the gospel, ye all are partakers of my grace. ⁸ For God is my record, how greatly I long after you all in the bowels of Jesus Christ. ⁹ And this I pray, that your love may abound yet more and more in knowledge and in all judgment; ¹⁰ That ye may approve things that are excellent; that ye may be sincere and without offence till the day of Christ; ¹¹ Being filled with the fruits of righteousness, which are by Jesus Christ, unto the glory and praise of God."

Here in this passage we find the faithfulness of God stated clearly. We can be confident of one very important thing: God is faithful to perform it. God is faithful to complete it. God can be trusted to be the finisher and captain of our faith. Hebrews 2:10 refers to the Lord Jesus Christ as such as it says, "*For it became him, for whom are all things, and by whom are all things, in bringing many sons unto glory, to make the captain of their salvation perfect through sufferings.*" The passage in Philippians declares that Jesus Christ, the captain of our salvation, is faithful but Paul then admonishes the church at Philippi to deal in issues that are spiritual, "*that ye may approve things that are excellent; that ye may be sincere without offence till the day of Christ.*" By implication, Paul is declaring Christ as faithful, but man as unfaithful, needing exhortation to be found faithful.

Kept by the power of God through faith unto salvation – 1 Peter 1. *³Blessed be the God and Father of our Lord Jesus Christ, which according to his abundant mercy hath begotten us again unto a lively hope by the resurrection of Jesus Christ from the dead, ⁴ To an inheritance incorruptible, and undefiled, and that fadeth not away, reserved in heaven for you, ⁵ Who are kept by the power of God through faith unto salvation ready to be revealed in the last time.*"

This is another passage that at first glance would indicate that salvation is secure. When you consider that there is no force in this existence that is stronger than the power of God, the result must be eternal security, right? Perhaps, not. Consider the statement in its entirety. The power of God is available to each and every believer ... but only through faith. Without the presence of faith, salvation is not possible. Without the faith covenant, you cannot, as II Corinthians 5:7 tells us, *"We walk by faith, not by sight."* A person who refuses to walk by faith cannot be covered through a faith covenant.

When a man walks down the aisle in a church and shakes hands with the preacher, he then states that he does believe that Jesus is the Christ. He goes on to be baptized and then begins a life of Christian service. But if he never goes from belief to faith, there is no contract, no covenant, of salvation. It cannot exist in the absence of faith. He can go through the process of baptism time and again, but without faith, there is nothing that suggests from Scripture that the man is saved. James, the Lord's half-brother, in Chapter 1 of his epistle speaks to the necessity of showing the evidence of the Christian re-birth and everlasting life, that faith without growth, being alone, is insufficient. We show the evidence through works that are the result of the change in our lives that Jesus Christ makes. We are not saved through our works - we are saved by grace through faith — but a true faith that permits God to work daily in our lives and through our lives for His glory. Never lose sight of the fact that God is the initiator of salvation (Romans 5:6-8), the sustainer of salvation (1st Peter 1:5) and the perfector of our salvation (Hebrews 2:10).

This gets right smack dab in the middle of the issue of pew potatoes. You know of whom I speak, for they are the ones who walk into a church on a Sunday morning with an attitude that says, **"I'm here, bless ME."**

They're the ones who come and go as the seasons change. They never get involved in ministry and, if you care to examine the tithe records, you will find that they rarely give to the Lord that which already belongs to Him. The idea that they can sit in a church service for Sunday after Sunday and have the Word of God not take any effect in their lives is because they are spiritually still dead. They were never truly saved in the first place. That's why they are not missed when they go into 'back-sliding mode', since they've never really been part of the family of God.

Now some may state that I am being judgmental. Perhaps that is true, except that in this case, I believe, that it is correct to righteously discern who is within and who is outside of the family of God (something that each pastor should discern). Some might look at this suggestion and say that it presents no third option and I would have to agree. To examine this paper at this point, you could suggest that it straddles the fence and does not suggest any additional insight to the debate. But let's go back and discuss those folk who were on the stony ground and the thorny ground. Let's do this so we can identify everyone in a church.

The '**thorny ground people**' are materialistic people who, like many of the Jews, want Christ to be an earthly ruler, a conquering hero, who will put them in a place of vast reward. They are encouraged by prosperity preachers who regularly say that all you need to do to get God's riches is to ask for them (and to send in a large donation to that man's ministry so that they would also pray for your blessing). They aren't just interested in keeping up with the Jones' family. They want to have so much wealth that it makes the Jones family and all other families jealous. Since man cannot serve two masters, their pursuit of material things leaves no room for the Lord, the study of His Word or a commitment to prayer. They are spiritually dead. Churches that are merely interested in their 'attendance numbers' permit and encourage (through the church's silence) pew potatoes to continue on their path of destruction. Those churches are just as wrong as the pew potatoes and will be held accountable by the Lord for their silence.

Or perhaps the '**thorny ground people**' can be placed into the group of people who find it easier to say they are only 'part-time' members of a church. This is an accurate description, since they spend most of the time in pursuing golf, fishing, softball, pageants, PTA, Rotary, Lion's Clubs, or even politics. They are consumed with seeking self-gratification in all of these activities. They have no interest in going to church as long as there's a bar-b-que going or a golf tournament or a skiing trip.

And then there are the '**stony ground people**'. These are the ones who have spent no time in the study of God's Word. They have so many activities going that they set aside no time for the Lord. They are the ones most likely to tell you that they were "not being fed" at their last church. Unfortunately, they wanted milk while the pastor wanted them to mature as Christians and fed them meat.

In Matthew 13, verses 6 & 7, the passage says that those who were in this group either withered away or they were choked. In essence, ***their faith died***. What does this do to the faith covenant? If a man no longer has faith in the covenant is the covenant of any effect? Can the man enjoy the blessings of the covenant? Can a righteous God give the same eternal reward to someone who does not possess faith? Some may choose to say that these were never '**really saved**', but is that position really valid? Can we say they were not saved or would it be just as easy to say that they lost their salvation? Simply because a person joins a church and is converted to a religion does not mean that they have been regenerated by the Holy Spirit. While you and I are not supposed to judge people, we are to be inspectors of fruit. Look at people's lives!

Chapter 16

A Sovereign God

Consider the idea of a person who possesses a 'free pass' to a major theme park. Since I live in Houston, Texas, I will use the Six Flags / Astroworld theme park as the example. Let's say that before I go to the park, I use the ticket to write down phone numbers. Or perhaps I've left it at home by mistake. Or maybe I just didn't care about the 'free pass' that I ***had***. Does this imply that the theme park has a responsibility to honor a 'free pass' that I have lost or misplaced or simply chosen no to use? Certainly not! People would never expect that to occur, although I have seen some who would plead for mercy. This is exactly the same idea of someone who simply went through the motions of Christianity having the same result of someone whose life was changed by the power of the blood of Jesus Christ.

And this brings us to the major point of all of this. Everything that has been written and prayed over has been stated in order to make the following statements.

1. God is faithful.
2. Man is not faithful.
3. The equation must balance.
4. The truth of Scripture must be in full and complete agreement.

If God is faithful and man is not, when there is any breakdown of the covenant it must be on the part of man. Psalm 94:11 tells us, "*The LORD knoweth the thoughts of man, that they are vanity."* If man is able to sustain salvation by his own actions, why would God go through the steps of sanctification? If God had no desire for man to change, why does the Lord chasten us? There must be a clear and concise answer. The answer, I believe is found in Philippians 2. This passage says, *"[12]Wherefore, my beloved, as ye have always obeyed, not as in my presence only, but now much more in my absence, **work out your own salvation with fear and trembling**. [13] For it is **God which worketh in you** both to will and to do of his good pleasure."* This passage is echoed in Ephesians 2. That passage says, *"[8] For by grace are ye saved through faith; and that not of yourselves: it is the gift of God: [9] Not of works, lest any man should boast. [10] For **we are his workmanship**, created in Christ Jesus unto good works, which God hath before ordained that we should walk in them."*

The only solution that I find is the **Third Option**. This is the only thing that allows the 'balancing act' to fit the nature of the Lord, the character of the Lord, the nature of man and the character of man. To establish the basis for this Third Option, let's examine the key points that must be satisfied.

The Sovereignty of God: One of the basic ideals of the Calvinist viewpoint relies heavily on the issue of God, as the Supreme Being of this entire universe, as the Eternal One who created all things, **and His absolute sovereignty over all things**. While a healthy respect for our Lord is appropriate, we need to be sure that we do not offend the **rights** of God. Let's go way back into the Book of Genesis, just to make

The Balancing Act

sure that nothing has been overlooked that has not been factored into the doctrinal position.

In Genesis 3, we have the account of the fall of man. Let's look carefully at the account because there is something that we must consider, that occurs after sin has been committed.

Genesis 3 *[8]And they heard the voice of the LORD God walking in the garden in the cool of the day: and Adam and his wife hid themselves from the presence of the LORD God amongst the trees of the garden. [9] And the LORD God called unto Adam, and said unto him, Where art thou? [10] And he said, I heard thy voice in the garden, and I was afraid, because I was naked; and I hid myself.*

We'll continue with this passage, but first ask if God was ignorant of Adam's transgression? Certainly not! If God is omniscient, and we certainly believe that He is, then He must have known already about the sin. I pose the question strictly to show that we are examining the character of the Lord correctly. Next, look at the next question that God asks.

Genesis 3 *[11]And he said, Who told thee that thou wast naked? Hast thou eaten of the tree, whereof I commanded thee that thou shouldest not eat? [12] And the man said, The woman whom thou gavest to be with me, she gave me of the tree, and I did eat.*

In all of Scripture, God never asks a question to which He does not already know the answer. Man tries to shift the blame to the woman. So God addresses the woman.

Genesis 3: [13] *And the LORD God said unto the woman, What is this that thou hast done? And the woman said, The serpent beguiled me, and I did eat.* [14] *And the LORD God said unto the serpent, Because thou hast done this, thou art cursed above all cattle, and above every beast of the field; upon thy belly shalt thou go, and dust shalt thou eat all the days of thy life*:

Talk about passing the buck! The blame was bouncing faster and more frequently than a worthless check. But God still knew the truth. Notice one thing that could have occurred and probably would have occurred with a less gracious God. Why didn't God simply annihilate the man, the woman and the serpent? If He is sovereign He should have done that, right? If God were sovereign, it would be His right? Correct? Be careful before you answer. Look carefully at the God's judgment.

Genesis 3: [15] *And I will put enmity between thee and the woman, and between thy seed and her seed; it shall bruise thy head, and thou shalt bruise his heel.* [16] *Unto the woman he said, I will greatly multiply thy sorrow and thy conception; in sorrow thou shalt bring forth children; and thy desire shall be to thy husband, and he shall rule over thee.* [17] *And unto Adam he said, Because thou hast hearkened unto the voice of thy wife, and hast eaten of the tree, of which I commanded thee, saying, Thou shalt not eat of it: cursed is the ground for thy sake; in sorrow shalt thou eat of it all the days of thy life;* [18] *Thorns also and thistles shall it bring forth to thee; and thou shalt eat the herb of the field; [19] In the sweat of thy face shalt thou eat bread, till thou return unto the ground; for out of it wast thou taken: for dust thou art, and unto dust shalt thou return. [20] And Adam called his wife's name Eve; because she was the mother of all living. [21] Unto Adam also and to his wife did the LORD God make coats of skins, and clothed them. [22] And the LORD God said, Behold, the man is become as one of us, to know good and evil: and now, lest he put forth his hand, and take also of the tree of life, and eat, and live for ever: [23] Therefore the LORD God sent him forth from the garden of Eden, to till the ground from whence he was taken. [24] So he drove out the man; and he placed at the east of the garden of Eden Cherubims, and a flaming sword which turned every way, to keep the way of the tree of life."*

When you see God's proclamation, many consider it to be a judgment of extreme love and caring for man's immortal soul. This is a valid observation in light of the Lord's character, but only when you do not truly consider the sovereignty of God. If God's sovereignty is truly complete, He should have wiped all three from their existence. Instead, He gave judgment to the precise limit of His authority over the earth. Look back in Genesis 1.

Genesis 1: [26] And God said, Let us make man in our image, after our likeness: and let them have dominion over the fish of the sea, and over the fowl of the air, and over the cattle, and over all the earth, and over every creeping thing that creepeth upon the earth.

Our righteous Lord gave dominion over the events that are played out on this earth to man. He then **voluntarily, in a free will decision**, minimized the extent to which He would involve Himself within time, as we know it (This also explains why bad things happen in this world, an entirely different subject). Once the Lord gave man dominion, He gave man responsibility. With responsibility comes accountability. In accountability, God's sovereignty covers mankind. This is why God limited His judgment temporally (within time) and temporarily (until the end of time) when man fell from grace by yielding to sin. God's sovereignty is not absolute and unconditional **at this time**.

This is a point that **must be clearly understood**. There must be no confusion on the issue of God's sovereignty. Man must not dictate the terms to God. God has done quite well without man's opinions that place the Lord in any questionable role. The correct answer is that **God chooses, not man, when He exerts His sovereignty**. That is the first of several points on which the Calvinists err by **assuming that God exerts His sovereignty in an inconsistent fashion** (where some are overwhelmed and others are not). Our Lord is gracious, but also righteous. Until the return and ultimate triumph of our Lord Jesus Christ, at which time all disobedience will cease – through the prevailing righteousness of Jesus Christ and through the sovereign will of God. Until Jesus Christ re-claims the dominion over all of the earth, God's sovereignty is not universally prevalent as long as sinful man retains the right to the same dominion that God gave man in the garden.

Predestination, foreknowledge, and election: The second error that we encounter is when we try to make three words mean the same thing. We covered this specific point previously as we listed proginosko (foreknow), proorizo (predestinate) and eklektos (elect). We need to understand that as the interpreters of Scripture, not the Author, chose words, they included some that perhaps you or I would have selected a different word. But where several translations are used, we find that the *Eight Translation New Testament* (Tyndale House Publishers, Inc., Wheaton, Illinois) does an adequate job by providing the King James Translation side by side with other translations and paraphrases. It's interesting when you do a comparison of the words that have been translated by the King James Version of the Bible. I have also included the New King James Version, also known as the *Open Bible* (Thomas Nelson Publishers, Nashville, Tennessee), for further consideration. Here is the result of the examination of the passages from Romans 8:29-33:

Bible	Proginosko	Proorizo	Eklektos
King James	Foreknow	Predestinate	Elect
Phillips Modern English	Fore-knowledge	Chose	Chosen
Revised Standard Version	Foreknew	Predestined	Elect
The Jerusalem Bible	Intended	Chose Specially	Chosen

The Living Bible	He Knew	Decided	Chosen
N.I.V.	Foreknew	Predestined	Chosen
Today's English Version	Had Chosen	Set Apart	Chosen People
Bible	Proginosko	Proorizo	Eklektos
New English Bible	Knew	Fore-ordained	Chosen Ones
New King James	Foreknew	Predestined	Elect

I believe that it is curious, at least, that in every translation or paraphrase there are different words used in each translation. The difficulty that I have with the argument of the idea of election based on foreknowledge is the position I have previously stated: where it give God the posture of a six year old, pouting and inviting only a few friends to a birthday party. This isn't just a six year old having a temper tantrum, we are discussing the Lord God, Most High! Therefore, although the Lord *could* chose people prior to the creation of this universe, it must occur in a manner that truly gives the Lord the full glory and honor that He so richly deserves. **_And it must be done with a reverence appropriate to the Lord_**.

Salvation & the Faith Covenant: Part of me wants to leave this item for my final point in this essay. But a more reasonable part of me simply wants to declare God's truth. That truth can be stated, as I have done previously, that we are indeed saved by grace through faith. The Bible is quite clear on this point, Acts 8,

Ephesians 2, Romans 5, etc. There are many examples of the faith covenant as the only medium and means of salvation. Romans 10:9-10 tells us, "*[9] That if thou shalt confess with thy mouth the Lord Jesus, and shalt believe in thine heart that God hath raised him from the dead, thou shalt be saved. [10] For with the heart man believeth unto righteousness; and with the mouth confession is made unto salvation.*" Belief with the heart and public confession of faith in Jesus Christ is a requirement to be saved. It is done exclusively in the name of Jesus Christ. Acts 4:12 states, "*Neither is there salvation in any other: for there is none other name under heaven given among men, whereby we must be saved.*" Having said this let me leave the issue of faith for the moment.

God's Grace and Limitations: I don't know about you, but I am offended when people begin to speak of God's grace being limited or inhibited. The apostle Paul was emphatic about not being responsible for inhibiting God's grace. In Galatians 2:21, Paul tells us, "*I do not frustrate the grace of God.*" As man contrives to deem 'limits' on the grace of God, for social or theological convenience, there can be no other result. Yet Paul's declaration in Galatians 2 gives heed to the limitless grace that **_can be poured out from the throne of grace_**. That is why the context of Paul's declaration reads, "*[20] I am crucified with Christ: nevertheless I live; yet not I, but Christ liveth in me: and the life which I now live in the flesh I live by the faith of the Son of God, who loved me, and gave himself for me. [21] I do not frustrate the grace of God: for if righteousness come by the law, then Christ is dead in vain.*" Since Paul is declaring himself as a believer and applying the need for all believers to place themselves in the same fashion, as channels of grace, not inhibiters of grace.

We should also discuss the impact of if there is a difference between 'general grace' and 'saving grace'. This difference appears to be the work of a group of people with far too much time on their hands. If God is the source of grace, who are we to 'segregate' what type of grace men can receive? How impertinent! Man should be far more humble than to attempt to diagnose the 'type' of grace that any man can receive. How can you begin to establish a basis for grace, which is God's unmerited favor or God's Riches At Christ's Expense? There is nothing in the intellect of man that should begin to fathom any difference between this concept of two types of grace. Perhaps Paul's indictment, as stated in Romans 3:19 should be applied, as we are told of our iniquity, when Paul tells us, "*Now we know that what things soever the law saith, it saith to them who are under the law: that every mouth may be stopped, and all the world may become guilty before God.*"

It is equally amazing that God's grace can be even discerned by man, yet it can be found sufficient in some case and insufficient in others. I am amazed that an omnipotent God would dare claim that omnipotence under such a circumstance. How could we even consider a 'god' who would have this failing characteristic? When we see the God of the Gospel we should hold to the word of Jesus Christ as He tells us in Luke 18:26-27, " [26] *And they that heard it said, who then can be saved?* [27] *And he said, the things which are impossible with men are possible with God.*" The truth of this statement is never clearer than dealing with the issue of salvation. We must see that if all things are indeed possible with God, then all of mankind ***can be redeemed***. Whether all of mankind will be redeemed is another matter entirely, but God has to provide the means for all to come to repentance or He becomes a 'country club god', serving the needs of a choice few.

Man's free will is not associated with salvation in any manner: Since I have spoken rather clearly on this point, I will not belabor the matter. Suffice it to say that man must respond to God or God cannot receive the glory. Man must have a choice or there cannot be obedience (and obedience is the purest form of worship). Free will on the part of man must be involved with the decision.

God cannot save all men and women and **God's plan of salvation did not include all of man**: We have looked at the intent of this type of doctrinal position as being founded on making the sacrifice of Christ a maximized event. There is honor in the intent of man, to say that Christ's death delivered all of those who were to be saved. Yet there is an inherent problem with this specific position. It is coupled with the provision that God, while still in a righteous fashion, **predestines a man or woman to an eternity in hell**. How can this be?

Look at the case of Adam and the fall from grace. Adam did only one thing wrong. He disobeyed a direct command from God. He did not steal. He did not commit adultery (That would have been tough since Eve was the only other woman living at this time). He did not kill. He did not bear false witness. Yet that one sin, of disobeying a direct order from the Lord was sufficient ground to send Jesus Christ to die on the cross. Adam did not gas Jews at Auschwitz. He did not kill Japanese people by dropping an atomic bomb on the cities of Hiroshima or Nagasaki. All Adam did was to forget, for just one instant, what God had told him not to do. That one transgression is all that it took for man to need Christ to provide atonement.

So when we see someone calling for Christ to save only a 'select group' while another is condemned to an eternity of torment, **we must ask 'How can this be**?' This hardly sounds like the same God who was willing to die for one simple forgotten command. It does not balance with the nature of Christ! It cannot be reconciled with what we know of the Father. Neither does it bear any common characteristic of the Comforter, The Holy Spirit.

Jesus' sacrifice is not completely successful because not all men will be saved: This is an interesting statement and one that I briefly spoke of previously. Consider a hostage situation. If, of thirteen men, three women and six children, only one man, two women and five children are rescued, is that a successful rescue mission? Are all rescue missions determined to be successful if not all return safely? What happens if, as occurred many times in World War I, World War II, the Korean War and the Vietnam War, a soldier chooses to remain behind? When do you consider the mission to be successful? That one man is redeemed is sufficient to honor God. That one soul is lost does nothing to diminish Christ's sinless life, His perfect death and His triumphant resurrection. We do not honor the Lord with an ideal of limited atonement. Jonathon Edwards, the great preacher, had this to say – "I go out to preach with two propositions in mind. First, everyone ought to give his life to Christ. Second, whether or not anyone gives Him his life, I will give Him mine."

People, who have tasted the goodness of the Lord, can reject the faith covenant and lose their salvation, with the result of spending eternity in the Lake of Fire: This is the point where all of the confusion is centered and all the debate is taken. Why? The answer lies in man's desire, not God's design, to hold a policy where some are just not worthy (or appear to be less unworthy) to receive God's grace. When you or I look at other men and women and then compare ourselves to those carnal mortals, we still miss the mark. We still sin and we do not progress onward to sanctification. Man's only comparison should be to the Lord Jesus Christ. He is the ***STANDARD*** by which we will ultimately be judged – whether in Christ or outside of Christ. This is the great error of the doctrinal point. We judge other men and women rather than discerning Spiritual fruit. Rather than discern the change that a personal relationship with Jesus Christ brings, and, in an attempt to make Scripture fit our chosen posture, we hold to either the position of having limited atonement or the possibility of losing salvation. By not discerning Spiritual fruit, we reject the only valid test criteria of a man's standing in Christ.

Dr. Daniel F. Beckley

Chapter 17

The Best Choice

Now, let's look at the two positions that are taken:

First – on the issue of limited salvation, we try to make the Lord fit into a certain criteria that cannot be jointly fit with His character and His nature. If a man adopts this posture, he sins through pride. He is stating that in God's creation of man and woman, some have more value than others. Some are not worthy of the Lord, but the person holding to the doctrine of limited atonement cannot possibly be part of the 'unsaved' group. They deign that they are worthy ... a position that smacks of superiority. It is impossible that God can be honored by anything that places other men and women into that inferior position.

Second – on the issue of losing salvation, those who hold to this position, generally speaking, are considering someone other than themselves. Others lose salvation while the one who holds this position is always safe and secure. They have no fear of losing salvation themselves, but everyone else is in mortal danger of their immortal soul.

To each of these positions, I suggest that the passage in Matthew 7:1-5 be read carefully. There we find, " [1] *Judge not, that ye be not judged.* [2] *For with what judgment ye judge, ye shall be judged: and with what measure ye mete, it shall be measured to you again.* [3] *And why beholdest thou the mote that is in thy brother's eye, but considerest not the beam that is in thine own eye?* [4] *Or how wilt thou say to thy brother, Let me pull out the mote out of thine eye; and, behold, a beam is in thine own eye?* [5] *Thou hypocrite, first cast out the beam out of thine own eye; and then shalt thou see clearly to cast out the mote out of thy brother's eye."* If we fail to evaluate our own position in light of the doctrine to which we have adopted, we do ourselves a great disservice.

So what is the answer? Look at the following table. It is simple in its merit, but it gives reason for serious contemplation of our own standing in Christ.

The Lord	Man
God is eternally faithful in all things.	Man is mortally unfaithful in all things.
Salvation is always secure with the Lord.	Salvation is not a guaranteed result.

There are several things that need to be considered about this brief table. The first thing is that the doctrinal positions of limited atonement and security in / losing of salvation look at only one side of this equation. The issue of limited atonement is man's attempt to define God as always 100% successful in everything that He does. The idea of losing salvation examines man's deficiencies and frailties. This table examines **both aspects, the Divine and the mortal**, side by side and in concert with each other. ***THIS IS WHAT NEEDS TO BE BALANCED***.

This, I believe is where mankind in general, and the various denominations that compose churches specifically, fail in their efforts to deal with the real issues. Salvation is secure in the Lord exclusively because God is always faithful. **He never fails**. He never breaks a promise. Within Christ, salvation is secure. Jesus said in John 10, "^{27} *My sheep hear my voice, and I know them, and they follow me*: ^{28} *And I give unto them eternal life; and they shall never perish, neither shall any man pluck them out of my hand.* ^{29} *My Father, which gave them me, is greater than all; and no man is able to pluck them out of my Father's hand.* ^{30} *I and my Father are one.*" We must engage in a diligent effort to be found as one of the Lord's flock. That requires self-examination and self-judgment, but, more importantly, when shown the deficiency by the Holy Spirit, we must change our actions. We must constantly pick the rocks, stones and thorns from the garden of our life that we may bear fruit more abundantly through Christ. That self-examination must occur so that we develop a humility that prevents us from judging others, but permits discernment of spiritual fruit.

Unfortunately, man is seldom faithful. Man has rarely held up his end of any contract voluntarily. Man must be coerced, under extreme penalty, before he will pay his taxes to the United States government. The due taxes are nominally taken from the citizens because we cannot be trusted to be faithful, not for our 'convenience', as most people would assume. Yet, in most cases, this lack of faithfulness appears to be true when pertaining to the issue of tithes and offerings to the Lord. Man is a steward of all that God has given him, yet man does not deal faithfully and honestly with the Lord. In Isaiah 64, we find " *⁴ For since the beginning of the world men have not heard, nor perceived by the ear, neither hath the eye seen, O God, beside thee, what he hath prepared for him that waiteth for him. ⁵ Thou meetest him that rejoiceth and worketh righteousness, those that remember thee in thy ways: behold, thou art wroth; for we have sinned: in those is continuance, and we shall be saved. ⁶ But we are all as an unclean thing, and all our righteousnesses are as filthy rags; and we all do fade as a leaf; and our iniquities, like the wind, have taken us away.*" Those 'filthy rags' are the putrid wrappings of a leper and that is precisely the nature of our good works – filthy and diseased rags.

So, where do we go from here? What is it that we have learned? We have seen that neither position, Calvinist nor Arminian, balances with Scripture. Neither position can stand the test of meeting the nature of God, the character of God, the nature of man and the character of man. Both have their merit, but both fail because they cannot pass the balancing act. They cannot pass muster on the requirements which doctrine must be based. We need to find that special balance that is from the Lord.

Once we can glimpse God's true position on issues of sovereignty, free will and other critical points, then and then only can we see the need to develop a **_Third Option_**, an alternative to the two conflicting positions.

The Balancing Act

As Joshua said in Joshua 24:15, *"And if it seem evil unto you to serve the LORD, choose you this day whom ye will serve; whether the gods which your fathers served that were on the other side of the flood, or the gods of the Amorites, in whose land ye dwell: but as for me and my house, we will serve the LORD."*

Man has always had to make choices. The difficult choices are usually delayed until the last possible moment. It was true in Joshua's time and it is still true today. The most likely position, balancing Scripture with natures and characters, can be stated as in the following table:

The Lord	Mankind
God calls man through His creation and His Word (Romans 1 & 2).	Man responds and, through a free will choice, acknowledges God's call (Psalm 111:10).
God calls man to repentance (II Chronicles 7:14).	Man must respond and see the need to repent (Psalm 14:2-3).
The Lord provides the Lamb of God for all men to receive as a free gift, by grace through faith (John 3:16-21).	Man answers and accepts the free gift of God, BUT THROUGH FAITH (Ephesians 2:8-10).
God's Spirit indwells man as a surety of God's promises (Romans 8:11).	Man must be led by the Spirit (Galatians 5:16).

The Lord	Mankind
The Holy Spirit begins regeneration (Romans 8:1-10).	Man either yields to the Spirit or he is only converted to a religion. Romans 8:13-14
The Holy Spirit teaches man to change his ways (Romans 8:12-14).	Man must respond in obedience (Romans 8:12-14)
God calls man to change. This is why God chastises man (Hebrews 12:6-8).	Man must change and be conformed to the image of Jesus Christ through the process of sanctification (Romans 8:29).
God wants man to look forward to our eternal reward in the kingdom (Matthew 6:19-21)	Man can make salvation of no effect through his lack of faith and trust in the Lord. (Hebrews 2:3-4)
God is faithful to provide salvation to faithful men and women who honor the covenant (Hebrews 6:9-20).	The covenant requires that man must be found faithful or else salvation is made of no effect (Hebrews 6:9-20).

This is not an instance of 'either / or'. Neither is it an attempt to placate the various factions, patting them on the back and whispering that they were so very close to God's truth. We have a moral and an ethical obligation to continue to seek God's truth. We need to engage in that search daily, trusting that God will willingly reward our search efforts.

Losing salvation or making it of no effect is what we have been discussing. There can be no denial that God always has wanted man to come to repentance. But like the man with the 'free pass', he can make the pass absolutely worthless if it is never redeemed. That would be the greatest shame of all. Not that man would choose temporal comfort in lieu of eternal blessing, but **_that man could taste the of the goodness of the Lord and still reject it_**. It is only how great an example of how depraved man really is. Jesus spoke to a young man one day and we see, "And when Jesus saw that he answered discreetly, he said unto him, Thou art not far from the kingdom of God. And no man after that durst ask him any question." To be so close but not yet in the kingdom of God is a sad circumstance.

Dr. Daniel F. Beckley

Chapter 18

The Best Option

One of the difficulties in presenting a third option relates to a question of arrogance and ego. There are some who are so self-assured, so full of themselves that they would never question what they have written. After all, they have studied the position to which they cling and clearly consider themselves to be the final arbiter. The problem is that in reality, the Lord has the final say on all matters. I am not so arrogant or egotistical to suggest that I have all of the right answers. I am, however, willing to continue my search until I breathe my last breath on this earth and step into the presence of my Lord and my God – at which time I will be humbled beyond my wildest imagination by the glory of Jesus Christ.

I would like to propose one last point to the reader and it relates to the sovereignty of God and why He would choose to only exhibit total sovereignty in eternity. It is this one point that asks you how to balance an omnipotent, omnipresent, omniscient and sovereign God with the free will expression of one mortal man. To truly consider this point, we must look back at the Garden of Eden – yes, that place where disobedience occurred and God gave the man, the woman and the serpent His Divine judgment for their actions.

Genesis 3 – "^{1}Now the serpent was more subtil than any beast of the field which the LORD God had made. And he said unto the woman, Yea, hath God said, Ye shall not eat of every tree of the garden? ^{2}And the woman said unto the serpent, We may eat of the fruit of the trees of the garden: ^{3}But of the fruit of the tree which is in the midst of the garden, God hath said, Ye shall not eat of it, neither shall ye touch it, lest ye die. ^{4}And the serpent said unto the woman, Ye shall not surely die: ^{5}For God doth know that in the day ye eat thereof, then your eyes shall be opened, and ye shall be as gods, knowing good and evil." In this instance where we know that Eve is deceived by the serpent, we find that Eve is seen as ignorant of God's Word. If we compare the words that she recites to the serpent we see that they are different from what the Lord God told Adam in Chapter 2, Verses 16 & 17 – "^{16}And the LORD God commanded the man, saying, Of every tree of the garden thou mayest freely eat: ^{17}But of the tree of the knowledge of good and evil, thou shalt not eat of it: for in the day that thou eatest thereof thou shalt surely die." Whether Adam put his 'spin' on God's Word or whether Eve was simply ignorant, she commits to the sin because she **_doubts God's Word_**! Even before she reached to touch the fruit, she doubts that God is telling her the truth. She doesn't correct the serpent.

Then, we have the sin issue made apparent for both Adam and Eve – "^{6}And when the woman saw that the tree was good for food, and that it was pleasant to the eyes, and a tree to be desired to make one wise, she took of the fruit thereof, and did eat, and gave also unto her husband with her; and he did eat. ^{7}And the eyes of them both were opened, and they knew that they were naked; and they sewed fig leaves together, and made themselves aprons."* **They are aware of their disobedience as well as their nakedness**. They are exposed for all to see.

Then God comes along, already aware of what has transpired – *"And they heard the voice of the LORD God walking in the garden in the cool of the day: and Adam and his wife hid themselves from the presence of the LORD God amongst the trees of the garden."* It was God's practice to walk and have full fellowship in the garden with man and because Adam and Eve are conscious of their sin – not just their nakedness. As God finally gets man and woman to respond, they try to shift the blame. Finally, the Lord issues His judgments.

First, we have the judgment of the serpent. *"[14]And the LORD God said unto the serpent, Because thou hast done this, thou art cursed above all cattle, and above every beast of the field; upon thy belly shalt thou go, and dust shalt thou eat all the days of thy life: [15]And I will put enmity between thee and the woman, and between thy seed and her seed; it shall bruise thy head, and thou shalt bruise his heel."*

Then we have the judgment of Eve, verse 15 – *"Unto the woman he said, I will greatly multiply thy sorrow and thy conception; in sorrow thou shalt bring forth children; and thy desire shall be to thy husband, and he shall rule over thee."*

We see the Lord's judgment of Adam in verses 17 to 19 – *"[17]And unto Adam he said, Because thou hast hearkened unto the voice of thy wife, and hast eaten of the tree, of which I commanded thee, saying, Thou shalt not eat of it: cursed is the ground for thy sake; in sorrow shalt thou eat of it all the days of thy life;* [18]*Thorns also and thistles shall it bring forth to thee; and thou shalt eat the herb of the field;* [19]*In the sweat of thy face shalt thou eat bread, till thou return unto the ground; for out of it wast thou taken: for dust thou art, and unto dust shalt thou return."*

Finally, we see them expelled from the garden – "[21]*Unto Adam also and to his wife did the LORD God make coats of skins, and clothed them.* [22]*And the LORD God said, Behold, the man is become as one of us, to know good and evil: and now, lest he put forth his hand, and take also of the tree of life, and eat, and live for ever.* [23]*Therefore the LORD God sent him forth from the garden of Eden, to till the ground from whence he was taken.* [24]*So he drove out the man; and he placed at the east of the Garden of Eden Cherubims, and a flaming sword which turned every way, to keep the way of the tree of life."*

After God sheds the blood of the animals, from which God clothes them and covers their shame, the Lord sends them forth from the garden to live out their days under the judgments pronounced earlier in the chapter. But there is a question that begs asking – Why? Why didn't God just annihilate them? Why let them continue to live?

Here is where we see the sovereignty of God exercised with restraint. God, in all His holiness and His righteousness, would be perfectly justified in blasting Adam and Eve from the face of not just the earth but of all existence. Yet He doesn't – for two reasons. One of the reasons has been a well-preached topic – the **PROMISE OF A SAVIOR**. The other reason is the point I want us to examine.

Consider why God would exercise restraint. What could possibly be the motive – other than that He said He would supply a Savior to bruise the head of the serpent? Certainly, it's not because God did not have the power. We are told, in Matthew 28:18, that *"all power in heaven and earth is given"* to the Lord Jesus Christ – so that eliminates the lack of power from the realm of possibilities.

It can't possibly be that God lacked the knowledge. We know from Psalm 104:24 tells us, *"O LORD, how manifold are thy works! in wisdom hast thou made them all: the earth is full of thy riches."*

So what could possibly have presented God with a reason not to annihilate Adam and Eve? **Clearly God can exercise His sovereignty any time He wants to, can't he**? We're only in Chapter 3 of the first book of the Bible and we have a real question about the Lord's sovereignty. Let's go back to Chapter 1 of the book of Genesis, to Verse 26, where the Lord decides to create man.

Genesis 1 – *"[26] And God said, Let us make man in our image, after our likeness: and let them have dominion over the fish of the sea, and over the fowl of the air, and over the cattle, and over all the earth, and over every creeping thing that creepeth upon the earth. [27] So God created man in his own image, in the image of God created he him; male and female created he them.*

> ²⁸*And God blessed them, and God said unto them, Be fruitful, and multiply, and replenish the earth, and subdue it: and have dominion over the fish of the sea, and over the fowl of the air, and over every living thing that moveth upon the earth.* ²⁹*And God said, Behold, I have given you every herb bearing seed, which is upon the face of all the earth, and every tree, in the which is the fruit of a tree yielding seed; to you it shall be for meat.* ³⁰*And to every beast of the earth, and to every fowl of the air, and to every thing that creepeth upon the earth, wherein there is life, I have given every green herb for meat: and it was so.* ³¹*And God saw every thing that he had made, and, behold, it was very good. And the evening and the morning were the sixth day.*"

The Lord decides to do several things:

1. The Lord **creates man in His own image**. This means we are fashioned in the same pattern as God, a trinity consisting of the body, soul (intellect) and spirit.

2. The Lord **charges man with dominion over all of the earth**. In giving dominion, this is God placing man in charge of all things, including two particular tasks (we'll look at this later).

3. With dominion comes the responsibility of stewardship – of the things placed under us and the things placed in our hands. This includes placing into subjection our bodies, our minds and our spirit – as faithful stewards of what the Lord has given us.

4. When all is said and done, God doesn't just say, "Its okay." He doesn't say, "Its good." God tells us that, "It was **VERY** good!" Everything the Lord has done is always 'very' good.

So what can we surmise from this? As the Lord gives man dominion, he delegated authority to man. Now we need to understand that temporal sovereignty is the domino over something and the authority to enforce your will. However, dominion is delegated to us by the Lord and, thus, we are accountable, through stewardship, for our actions.

Further, once the Lord gave man dominion over the earth – God's direct judgments were suspended. God could change the rulings, but not the rules. He could no longer 'zap' Adam and Eve out of existence because He had delegated the authority and the management over the earth to Adam.

Yet it must be stated that we are still accountable to the sovereign God of this universe. If we look at the specific judgments that the Lord gave in Genesis 3, all of them we promises – promises of hard work for the man, pain for the woman and the ultimate defeat for the serpent. God's judgments fit perfectly with His prior actions.

Now, we must ask whether these actions detract from the sovereignty of God. Does it? The answer is a resounding "**NO**!" The reason is that God transcends His creation. We are in 'time' while the Lord is in 'eternity'. We exist within the limits of this feeble mortality while God transcends His creation and this is the key to understanding how God can still be sovereign even when we express our free will through our choices. We are still accountable to our Creator, our Lord, and our Sovereign.

I would hope that you would examine the writings carefully and prayerfully. I do not suggest that I have all of the answers. But the words of Jesus keep echoing in my ears, from John, Chapter 5. In verse 39, Jesus was speaking to the Pharisees when he told them, "***Search the scriptures***; *for in them ye think ye have eternal life: and they are they which testify of me."* Jesus commands even those who have studied Scripture for a living to continue to search the Scriptures. We think we have eternal life so we ***must continue to search the Scriptures***. We think we know of the things that testify of Jesus Christ, so we must ***continue to search the Scriptures***! Hold salvation so close that your faith never fades and your desire to search the Scripture for God's truth never fails.

Chapter 19

Afterward

Curiosities and conflicts present themselves as we move through this temporal existence. Some see these as things that cannot be resolved. Others see them as tragic events that are beyond their comprehension or reach. Still there is a group that persists in seeking ultimate truth with tireless efforts – knowing that God is still sovereign and we'll see the truth if we passionately seek it.

Calvinism v. Arminianism is just one of these matters that people either ignore or pursue with a vengeance. The whole point of this book isn't whether John Calvin or Jacobus Arminius is right. It isn't about whether I'm right. It about getting closer to God's Truth, not man's truth.

If this book inspires or incites you to search the Scriptures more closely, to read God's Word more abundantly, or develop a more personal relationship with Jesus Christ, then all of the research, study and writing has been worth it.

After all, it's not about us.